This book belongs to

____

a woman who desires to reflect the heart of Jesus

GROWTH & STUDY GUIDE

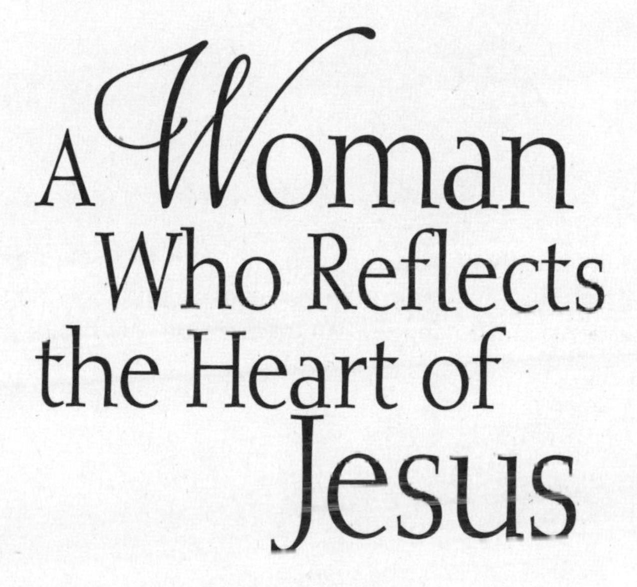

Elizabeth George

HARVEST HOUSE PUBLISHERS

EUGENE, OREGON

Cover by Dugan Design Group, Bloomington, Minnesota

Cover photo © Shaun Egan / The Image Bank / Getty Images

Acknowledgments

As always, thank you to my dear husband, Jim George, MDiv, ThM, for your able assistance, guidance, suggestions, and loving encouragement on this project.

A WOMAN WHO REFLECTS THE HEART OF JESUS GROWTH AND STUDY GUIDE

Published by Harvest House Publishers
Eugene, Oregon 97402
www.harvesthousepublishers.com

ISBN 978-0-7369-1477-2

Printed in the United States of America

10 11 12 13 14 15 16 17 18 / BP-SK / 10 9 8 7 6 5 4 3 2 1

Contents

From My Heart to Yours

If you know Jesus, I'm sure your deepest desire is to become more like Him. What a worthy life goal! As I prepared this growth and study guide, I had you in my mind and heart as I worked hard to make these lessons helpful, practical, and life-changing. It is my prayer that as you step into this incredible study of 30 of Jesus' sterling character qualities that you will grow spiritually and experience the dynamic change only He can bring about.

Change Is Coming

The lessons in this growth and study guide are easy to follow and do. You'll need a copy of *A Woman Who Reflects the Heart of Jesus,* your Bible, and a heart ready to learn how Jesus treated people, what kept Him focused, and how to live in a way that pleases God. As you use this growth and study guide, you get to set your own pace. You can enjoy one quality a day, or one a week, or find a rhythm that fits your lifestyle. You'll start each lesson by reading the chapter in the main book. Then, as you work through the questions, insights, additional scriptures, and the reflections on your heart in this growth and study guide, you'll gain a better understanding of the truths found in the Bible that can help make you more like Jesus. And best of all, you'll become a dazzling reflection of Him to a watching world. Although this may sound almost impossible, as you progress on your own 30-day journey, you'll surprise yourself as you are being transformed one character quality at a time.

The Advantages of Group Study

You will grow spiritually as you work your way through and apply the biblical principles presented in this growth and study guide, but I urge you to share this rich and life-changing journey with others—your friends, your neighbors, your Sunday school class, your Bible study. No matter how small or large the group, the personal care and interest that is shared will be uplifting and supportive. Your sisters in Christ will pray for you and you for them. You'll have a mutual exchange of experiences. And you'll have accountability, along with some healthy peer pressure. This will help motivate you to do the lessons and experience glorious spiritual growth! You'll enjoy sweet, sweet encouragement as you share God's Word with one another and stimulate one another to greater love and good works.

If you feel guided by God to lead a study group, I've included a section in the back of this study guide entitled "Leading a Bible Study Discussion Group." This practical, hands-on information... and more...is also available on my website:

www.ElizabethGeorge.com

Reaping the Benefits of Walking in Jesus' Steps

There is no way to list all the benefits that await you through this study of Jesus! You'll love revisiting your favorite scenes from His life. You'll delight in discovering new truths about Him. You'll hear His very own words and instructions from the Gospels. And, by His grace and with His help, you will grow to know Him more intimately and reflect Him more accurately—in a way that glorifies Him. I'm praying for you!

In His everlasting love,

Elizabeth George

Day 1

Approachable

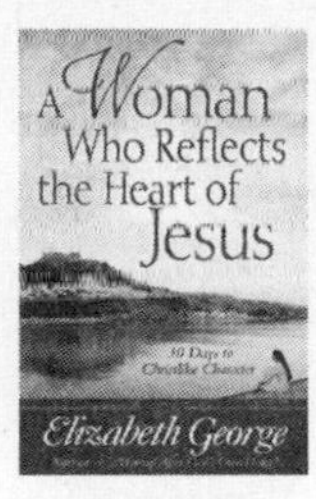

In your copy of *A Woman Who Reflects the Heart of Jesus,* read the chapter entitled "Approachable." What encouraged you the most about your journey to Christlike character, and why?

What challenged you the most, and why?

Jesus Shows Us the Way

Approachable to the Outcast

Read Mark 1:40-42 and detail the actions of...

The leper: What did the leper say, and how did he qualify his request (verse 40)?

Jesus: Describe His heart response (verse 41)—

His physical response (verse 41)—

His verbal response (verse 41)—

What was the result (verse 42)?

Reflecting On Your Heart

"Your Savior didn't allow the dictates of His society to keep Him from projecting an image that He was approachable." Search your heart and your attitudes toward others during the past week. How did your actions demonstrate you could be easily approached by friends, associates, strangers, and even "outcasts"? Also note any changes you absolutely must make.

Approachable to the Hopeless

Read Mark 2:1-12. What did the four friends expect as they brought their hopeless friend to Jesus (verses 3-4)?

Describe their determination to bring their friend to Jesus (verse 4).

What was Jesus' first response (verse 5)?

How did Jesus affirm His ability to forgive sin (verses 10-11)?

Reflecting On Your Heart

"Jesus teaches His followers to be careful not to allow crowds, packed schedules, and busyness to get in the way of people who truly need help." What can you do to be more aware of the needs of the "hopeless" who come across your path each day?

Approachable to the Concerned

Read Matthew 8:5-13. This is such a touching example of a man's need and Jesus' willingness to assist. What do you learn in verses 5-8 about the centurion's attitude...

toward his servant?

toward Jesus?

toward himself?

What do you learn about Jesus from His response to this man, to his need, and to the interruption?

How was Jesus willing to go "the extra mile" to take care of this need (verse 7)?

Reflecting On Your Heart

"Anything and everything can be seen as an inconvenience if you want it to be." Do you need to build a "flex quotient" into your day? Think of at least three ways you can respond more like Jesus when you are approached by someone with a burden of concern.

Approachable to the Unimportant

We can only hope the disciples finally caught on to Jesus' approachability! Read Matthew 19:13-15. Quickly note the actions of those involved:

The adults—

The children—

The disciples—

The Lord—

What a tender scene—except for the disciples' mistreatment of those eager to be near Jesus. How do you generally respond to the approaches of someone unknown and seemingly unimportant to you, and how do Jesus' actions inspire you?

Approachable to the Outsiders

Read Mark 7:24-30. Imagine the heartache this mother endured! What was her request (verse 26), and Jesus' initial answer (verse 27)?

This woman already knew she was an "outsider" (verse 28), yet she persisted. How did Jesus minister to this foreign woman, and what does He model for you?

Approachable to the Insincere

Read Mark 10:17-22. Fast-forward to verse 22 and note the evidence of this rich young man's insincerity.

Before this event took place, Jesus knew the eventual outcome of this encounter. Yet how did He treat this man when he approached Him? (Note at least three signs of Jesus' concern for this young man.)

Reflecting the Heart of Jesus

Read this final section in your book again. As you consider your character, jot down two or three changes or actions that would cause you to be more approachable to people and better reflect the heart of Jesus.

~ A Prayer to Pray ~

What can you add to the prayer in your book that will more specifically describe your desire to be more approachable?

Day 2

Available

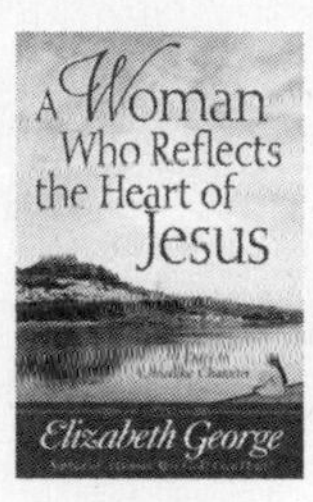

In your copy of *A Woman Who Reflects the Heart of Jesus,* read the chapter entitled "Available." What encouraged you the most about your journey to Christlike character, and why?

What challenged you the most, and why?

Jesus Shows Us the Way

Describe the difference between *approachable* and *available* as stated in your book.

Write out Matthew 20:28.

How does Matthew 20:28 describe Jesus' availability?

Give Me a Drink

Scan John 4:1-26. List several ways you see Jesus being available and reaching out to this Samaritan woman.

Reflecting On Your Heart

What do you see Jesus doing that you can imitate this week to be more available to share the "good news" with people you come in contact with?

Everyone Is Looking for You

Read Mark 1:29-39 and jot down the ways Jesus ministered to the different people around Him. Then describe a memorable hectic day of activity in your life. How did you view and treat the people involved in that busy day?

Note the steps Jesus took to prepare Himself for the next day's people and events (verse 35).

Reflecting On Your Heart

Did you notice these words? "You can't go every place or minister to every need." Praying helped Jesus know where to put His time and effort. Think about your tomorrow. List several things you can do to get a handle on it before it arrives.

While He Spoke...

Read Matthew 9:14-22. Briefly state what Jesus was talking about in verses 14-17.

According to verses 18-19, who arrived and interrupted Jesus' teaching, and what was Jesus' response?

Jesus was on His way to help. What do you learn from...

verse 20?

verse 21?

verse 22?

Now read the same account in Mark 5:35-43. Make a list of the people who were affected by Jesus' availability.

Reflecting On Your Heart

Now for you! List those who were affected by your availability yesterday. Then note any adjustments you may want to make for tomorrow. Remember, "at the end of a day of assisting others, people are helped and miracles happen—not the kinds of miracles Jesus executed, but miracles of hope and assurance, of love and comfort."

Your Brother Will Rise Again

Read John 11:1-23. What does verse 8 report as one problem Jesus would risk by helping Lazarus?

Jesus was available to minister to the needs of others, no matter what the risk or cost. How does His example encourage you in your ministry and give you confidence?

I Must Stay at Your House

After reading Luke 19:1-10, jot down the efforts Zacchaeus made to catch a glimpse of Jesus (verses 3-4).

What did Jesus do to indicate He was available even though He was on His way to another destination (verse 5)?

In your own words, why is it important for you to be available to others?

Reflecting the Heart of Jesus

Read this final section in your book again. As you consider your character, jot down two or three changes or actions that would cause you to be more available to people and better reflect the heart of Jesus.

~ A Prayer to Pray ~

What can you add to the prayer in your book that will more specifically describe your desire to be more available?

Day 3

Compassionate

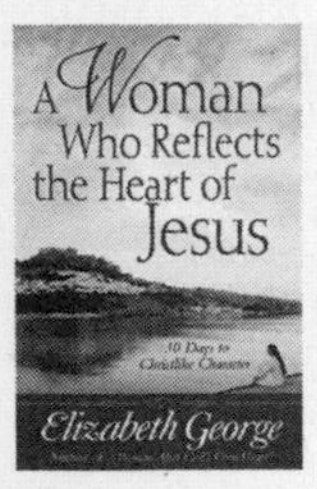

In your copy of *A Woman Who Reflects the Heart of Jesus,* read the chapter entitled "Compassionate." What encouraged you the most about your journey to Christlike character, and why?

What challenged you the most, and why?

Jesus Shows Us the Way

Using a dictionary, define *compassion.*

The Displays of Compassion

SCENE 1

Read Luke 5:12-15 and compare it to Mark 1:40-45. Note differences in the descriptions of the two accounts.

How does a comparison of these two accounts further display Jesus' compassion?

SCENE 2

Read Mark 6:30-32 and describe Jesus' reason for concern for His men.

Which people are the closest to you, and what can you do to show the same brand of compassion Jesus did?

SCENE 3

Read Mark 6:33-34 and describe what happened as Jesus tried to get His disciples away from the crowds to rest.

What was His first concern for the multitudes (verse 34)?

What was the disciples' "quick fix" to the problem (verse 36)? (Oops! Have you ever done this to your family?)

What was Jesus' compassionate solution to the people's need for food (verse 37)?

The Model of Compassion

Read the first paragraph of this section again, then briefly jot down the actions of compassion.

In your estimation, which action of compassion is the most important, and why?

Observe Jesus' compassion as you look up these additional passages:

Matthew 9:36—

Matthew 14:14—

Matthew 20:34—

Mark 5:19—

Luke 7:13—

Jesus saw a need and went about meeting that need. Compassion, unfortunately, is a little more difficult for us. We are usually more concerned about our own needs than the needs of others. What can you do to give compassion a more prominent place in your life? List at least three actions you can take to nurture compassion:

—

—

—

Reflecting the Heart of Jesus

Read this final section in your book again. As you consider your character, jot down two or three changes or actions that would help you to show more compassion to people and better reflect the heart of Jesus.

~ A Prayer to Pray ~

What can you add to the prayer in your book that will more specifically describe your desire to be more compassionate?

Day 4

Confident

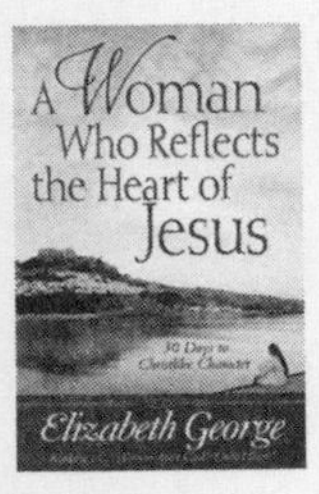

In your copy of *A Woman Who Reflects the Heart of Jesus*, read the chapter entitled "Confident." What encouraged you the most about your journey to Christlike character, and why?

What challenged you the most, and why?

Jesus Shows Us the Way

What were the two kinds of trust described in this section of the book?

—

—

I Must Be About My Father's Business

Even at an early age Jesus had great confidence. Read Luke 2:41-51 and describe the source of Jesus' confidence.

Reflecting On Your Heart

"Trusting in yourself is shaky ground. Trust instead in the rock that is solid, in Jesus Christ." There's no reason to be anxious about your routine, everyday activities. How does Proverbs 3:5-6 give you confidence as you follow its instructions?

Do Not Fear

Read Matthew 10:16-31. Jesus' disciples would (and you will, too) face persecution for their faith in Christ. As you read Jesus' talk to the disciples, note His advice in the following verses:

Verse 26—

Verse 28—

Verse 31—

What is Jesus' message to your heart as you prepare to handle persecution?

Reflecting On Your Heart

"Times of trouble will come, but rather than cowering in fear, have the confidence to trust your all-wise and loving heavenly Father." How does the truth of John 3:16 give you confidence as you face each day of challenges?

Believe in Me

Get John 14:1-3 firmly fixed in your mind and heart. Then look up the word *believe* in a dictionary, and write a brief definition below.

In the following verses, what is Jesus asking His disciples to believe?

Verse 1—

Verse 2—

Verse 3—

Reflecting On Your Heart

"If Jesus is your Savior, then you…have hope for the future. Whatever might happen from now till death, it doesn't really matter… Because you have placed your trust in a strong and mighty Savior." Look again at John 14:1-3. Which promise or truth fortifies your heart with confidence as you look to the future?

Take This Cup Away from Me

Take a look again at Luke 22:39-46. Briefly describe the setting and Jesus' agony.

What appears to have settled the conflict going on in Jesus' heart as He faced His encounter with the cross (verse 42)?

What agony is present in your heart today or at this season of your life? What tactics can you copy from Jesus' style of crisis management?

—

—

Reflecting On Your Heart

"Just as Jesus experienced, there are times when you have a difficult and costly decision to make...follow Jesus' example. Take your questions, fears, and reluctance to the Father in prayer. Reaffirm your willingness to do what's right." How do the teachings of John 14:15, 23, and 24 help you to do what's right?

Why is knowing and doing God's will vital to confident living, especially when you must make difficult choices?

You Shall Receive Power

As you read Acts 1:8, realize it was Jesus' last earthly promise before returning to heaven. What was His promise, and what were the disciples to do after Jesus' promise was fulfilled?

What served as proof that this promise was accomplished in the disciples...

in the way they behaved (Acts 4:13)?

in the way they ministered (Acts 4:31)?

You too have received the power of the Holy Spirit. How should that affect your confidence level...

in life in general?

in ministry?

in the face of opposition?

Reflecting the Heart of Jesus

Read this final section in your book again. As you consider your character, jot down two or three changes or actions that would cause you to show more confidence and better reflect the heart of Jesus.

~ A Prayer to Pray ~

What can you add to the prayer in your book that will more specifically describe your desire to have more confidence?

Day 5

Courageous

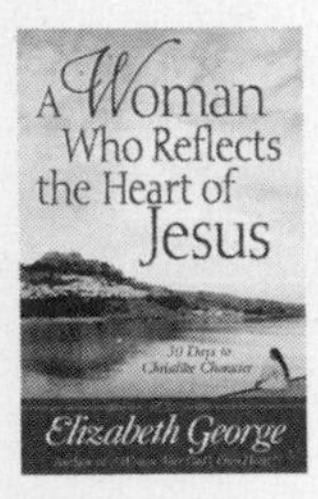

In your copy of *A Woman Who Reflects the Heart of Jesus*, read the chapter entitled "Courageous." What encouraged you the most about your journey to Christlike character, and why?

What challenged you the most, and why?

Before we move into the life of Jesus, read Joshua 1:1-9 and take a brief look at courage in the life of Joshua in the Old Testament. List the verses in which God spoke to Joshua about courage.

What did God say each time about courage?

What was the ultimate reason that Joshua could be courageous (verse 9)?

Reflecting On Your Heart

"Step One to gaining courage is realizing that fear is natural, whereas the presence of God right beside you, all the time, is supernatural." Compare Joshua 1:9 to the words Jesus spoke to the disciples—and ultimately to us today—in Matthew 28:20.

What was God's promise to Joshua?

And Jesus' promise to His followers?

And what is their message to your heart?

Jesus Shows Us the Way

Read this section in your book again. Why is the level of your courage so closely connected with your trust in Jesus?

Here are a handful of definitions of courage: "Courage is bravery. It's the power to do something in the face of fear. It's also the ability to act on beliefs despite danger or disappointment. Courage also gives you great strength in the face of pain or grief." How do these insights fortify you?

He Drove Them All Out of the Temple

Read and compare the two incidents described in John 2:13-19 and Matthew 21:12-13, where Jesus courageously drove money changers out of the temple. At what point in Jesus' ministry did each take place?

John 2:13-19—

Matthew 21:12-13—

Note the additional details provided in John's account—

There is a time and a place for the kind of courage Jesus exhibited in a situation where something is clearly wrong. But in general, how does God want you to live day by day, according to 1 Peter 3:4?

He Overcame the World

Pay close attention to John 16:28-33. Courage is not the absence of fear. Fear is normal. Courage is facing your fears. What was Jesus' prediction and concern for His disciples in verses 32 and 33?

What comforting information did Jesus want the disciples to know about their future (verse 33)?

What courage can you draw from knowing that Jesus has "overcome the world"?

Reflecting On Your Heart

"Someday—maybe even today—you will need courage for the tribulations Jesus said will come your way." Are you facing any sort of tribulation today? This week? How does knowing that Jesus is present with you and has already defeated the sources of evil in this world give you the courage and ability to face your problems and be an overcomer?

What instruction do these psalms give you for your times of fear and tribulation?

Psalm 27:1—

Psalm 56:3 and 11—

His Soul Was Exceedingly Sorrowful

After reading Matthew 26:36-44 and Luke 22:39-46, describe Jesus' anguish in the garden.

What words did Jesus repeat that helped Him keep His focus on the cross (Matthew 26:39,42,44)?

Others Show Us the Way

The Women at the Cross

Look for yourself at Matthew 27:54-56. We can only imagine that the women at the cross were fearful, yet they were faithful to do what needed to be done for their friend Jesus. Where could their courage have come from according to...

1 John 4:18?

2 Timothy 1:7?

What does their courage teach you about handling your hard times?

Reflecting On Your Heart

"Faith in Jesus is always the antidote for fear." Faith in Jesus fights fears. Name several of your fears.

Now ask yourself: "Are any of these issues too much for an all-powerful God to deal with?" Because the answer is obviously no, what are your plans for handing your fears over to Jesus?

The Man Who Asked for the Body of Jesus

For a portrait of courage, enjoy Luke 23:50-54 and John 19:38-42. As you read, note this man's acts of courage.

Joseph of Arimathea was willing to risk everything for Jesus at the time of His death. How does this man's courage help you with any fears you have of being closely identified with Jesus?

Reflecting the Heart of Jesus

Read this final section in your book again. As you consider your character, jot down two or three changes or actions that would cause you to be more courageous and better reflect the heart of Jesus.

~ A Prayer to Pray ~

What can you add to the prayer in your book that will more specifically describe your desire to be more courageous?

Day 6

Disciplined

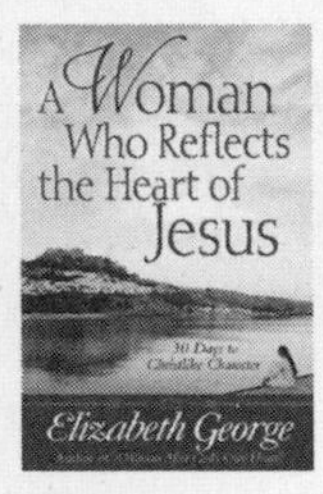

In your copy of *A Woman Who Reflects the Heart of Jesus*, read the chapter entitled "Disciplined." What encouraged you the most about your journey to Christlike character, and why?

What challenged you the most, and why?

Jesus Shows Us the Way

It Is Written...

Read Matthew 4:1-11 and record each of the three temptations Jesus faced and His responses:

The Temptation	*Jesus' Response*

Reflecting On Your Heart

In times of temptation, "you can call on God. You can tap into His power and His powerful Word for the discipline and self-control... you need." You can look to Jesus for help through His example and prayer. Can you identify a major area of temptation for you? How do you plan to fight back the next time you are tempted?

He Departed to a Solitary Place

Take a look at Mark 1:21-34, a day in Jesus' busy life. Note the variety of activities Jesus engaged in during this one day.

How did Jesus decide what to do the next day (verse 35)?

Verse 35 describes the choices Jesus made to enjoy a time of prayer. Note them here.

Reflecting On Your Heart

"Maintaining spiritual disciplines is a choice. You choose to do what you believe is important." What better choices can you make this week to be more faithful in prayer?

He Rebuked Them

Take a look at Luke 9:51-56. According to verses 51-52, what was happening in Jesus' life, and what assignment did He give to some of His disciples?

Note the response of the people to Jesus and the disciples—and the disciples' response to the people! How did the disciples want to handle the rejection of Jesus (verse 54)?

What was Jesus' reply to the disciples...and to you (verse 56)?

Reflecting On Your Heart

"How do you respond to rebuffs?" Discipline is always in order for a Christian. Can you point to an area in which you tend to lose it and give in to emotions, anger, or aggression? How do Jesus' words help you to reel in your emotions?

Others Show Us the Way

Blessed Is Your Discernment

Read 1 Samuel 25 and note the actions and attitudes of...

Nabal—

David—

By contrast, consider the actions and attitudes of Abigail. How do you see her discipline in these areas?

Disciplined emotions—

Disciplined mind—

Disciplined speech—

Disciplined organizational skills—

In my book *Walking with the Women of the Bible*,* I write about Abigail's "Breathtaking Character." Which facets of her disciplined character do you need to pay more attention to, and what one thing will you do about it this week?

* Elizabeth George, *Walking with the Women of the Bible* (Eugene, OR: Harvest House Publishers, 2008), p. 164.

She Took of Its Fruit and Ate

To view a woman not so disciplined, read Genesis 3:1-6. Notice the areas in which Eve lacked discipline. Then pick an area in which you tend to find yourself weak or easily tempted. Make a plan for strengthening that weakness, and follow through on it. (That's what discipline would do.)

Things to Remember About Discipline

Consider the facts about discipline in this section of your book. To make progress, which fact needs your immediate attention?

Reflecting the Heart of Jesus

Read this final section in your book again. As you consider your character, jot down two or three changes or actions that would cause you to be more disciplined and better reflect the heart of Jesus.

~ A Prayer to Pray ~

What can you add to the prayer in your book that will more specifically describe your desire to be more disciplined?

Day 7

Faithful

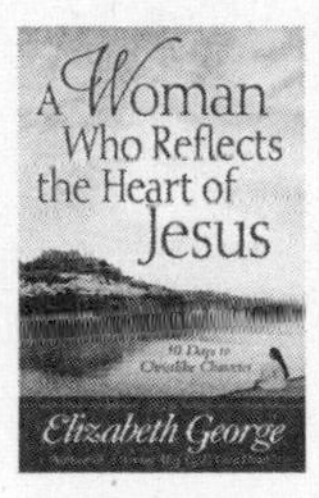

In your copy of *A Woman Who Reflects the Heart of Jesus*, read the chapter entitled "Faithful." What encouraged you the most about your journey to Christlike character, and why?

What challenged you the most, and why?

Jesus Shows Us the Way

I Have Finished the Work

Read John 4:34 and 17:4. What word is repeated in each verse, and what is said about it?

Now read 1 Timothy 3:11. List the four character qualities God desires in you as a woman, and circle the final one.

1.

2.

3.

4.

Jesus knew God's will for His life and faithfully pursued it. According to Titus 2:3-5, what are some of God's purposes for you?

1.

2.

3.

4.

5.

6.

7.

8.

9.

10.

Circle or check those areas that fall into the "needs improvement in faithfulness" category. And don't forget to give thanks to God for progress, improvement, and His faithful promise to finish the good work He has begun in you (Philippians 1:6)!

Pray and Do Not Lose Heart

From your Bible copy the words in Luke 18:1 that convey the reason Jesus spoke His parable and the importance of being faithful in prayer.

Like the Lord, you have a busy life, important events that require your time and energy, people who need your prayers, and maybe even a few enemies. Look for yourself at Jesus' solution to these life situations. Note also, in each instance, the message to your heart and your situation.

Mark 1:16-39—

Matthew 26:39-42—

John 17:1-5 (for Himself)—

John 17:20-26 (for you and all believers)—

Luke 23:32-34—

Those Whom You Gave Me I Have Kept

Look again at John 17, at verses 6-19, where we witness Jesus faithfully praying for others. Jesus shows us His love and concern for His disciples, including us. He also shows us how to pray for those we love. As you read, take notes on what Jesus prayed for. And don't forget to pray in these ways for your family, loved ones, and fellow believers.

Reflecting On Your Heart

"God asks for your faithfulness." In what key area of your life do you see a greater need for faithfulness? Share one thing you've done or are doing about it.

As a "grace note," look at these bonus verses to realize the divine help God has given you to enable your faithfulness.

John 14:16-17—

Galatians 5:22-23—

Honor Your Father and Your Mother

The Bible teaches us that family is important. Make notes as you see it for yourself in...

Exodus 20:12—

Matthew15:4—

Read John 19:25-27. In that passage, Jesus models faithfulness to family for us. Where was Jesus when this scene occurred?

As you pray about your parents, children, and family, how can you reach out to them this week? Check in with them? Honor them?

Reflecting the Heart of Jesus

Read this final section in your book again. As you consider your character, jot down two or three changes or actions that would cause you to become more faithful in all things and better reflect the heart of Jesus.

~ A Prayer to Pray ~

What can you add to the prayer in your book that will more specifically describe your desire to be more faithful?

Day 8

Focused

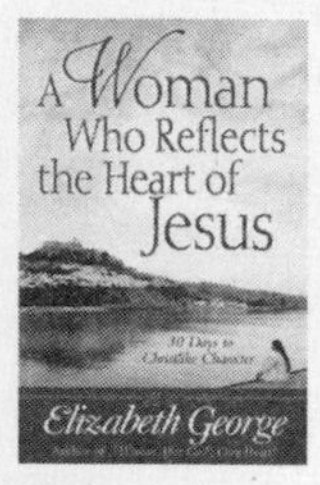

In your copy of *A Woman Who Reflects the Heart of Jesus*, read the chapter entitled "Focused." What encouraged you the most about your journey to Christlike character, and why?

What challenged you the most, and why?

Jesus Shows Us the Way

There's no way to even *think* Jesus aimed at nothing or lived an aimless life without focus! He perfectly modeled focus as He devoted Himself to living out God's will. As you work your way through this lesson, note the practices that led to Jesus' living out God's purpose for Him.

Jesus Himself Began His Ministry

Jesus prepared—This section of your book gives you some idea of the progression of Jesus' preparation. Glance over it again, then read Matthew 3:13-17. What was Jesus' final step of preparation, and how did the Father respond?

Reflecting On Your Heart

"To live with purpose means to focus your heart, time, energies, and priorities. It calls for taking advantage of each day." What are you aggressively doing to prepare for future service to God and the people in your life? Then share some of your plans for further preparation.

My present preparation—

My plans for future preparation—

While He Prayed...

Jesus prayed—The thread of Jesus' faithfulness to prayer is woven throughout the Gospels. It's no wonder that He prayed as He entered into His formal ministry. Do you want to know God's will? What does Mark 11:24 advise?

Reflecting On Your Heart

"As you steadily make prayer a habit, you will discover God's plan for your life." While Jesus prayed, heaven opened and the Father spoke. This exact scenario won't happen to you, but when you focus on being faithful in prayer, God will lead and guide you into the path of His purpose. Answer yes or no to the following:

Do you have a prayer list?

Are your goals and dreams on that list?

Are you praying through your list regularly?

What are your plans to focus more intently on God's purposes for you?

He Chose Us in Him

Jesus planned—He planned, and you were blessed as a result. Each day Jesus was focused, on track, and moving forward toward God's will and purpose. As you read Luke 13:32-33, what do you learn about Jesus' plan—and timetable—for going to the cross?

He Steadfastly Set His Face to Go to Jerusalem

Jesus proceeded—Read Luke 9:51. What is said about Jesus' determination in following through on God's will and plan?

Reflecting On Your Heart

"Jesus was determined to proceed to Jerusalem in spite of what He knew was waiting for Him." How's your resolve, your focus? Would the words *steadfast*, *determined*, and *focused* describe your forward movement toward God's will? If so, pray as you proceed. If not, try to pinpoint any obstacles. It may help to note them here. Then pray for God's power and grace to focus and keep moving toward what matters.

The Angels Ministered to Him

The Father provided—God provided for Jesus when He was tempted. Read these thrilling incidents of God's provision for Jesus, and note the nature of the temptation and God's provision in...

Mark 1:12-13—

Luke 22:39-44—

What was Jesus' advice to His disciples—and you—about temptation in verse 40?

Now read 1 Corinthians 10:13 in your Bible. What is God's promise to you regarding temptation?

Reflecting On Your Heart

"Through prayer, the assistance of God's Word, and support from others, God provides the way for you to remain faithful when you are tempted." Are you neglecting any of these three provisions God has made for you? What are your plans for filling in any gaps?

The Father's provision for all your needs—Read Philippians 4:11-13 and 19. What did Paul know about God's provision after focusing on serving the Lord for 20-plus years?

Reflecting On Your Heart

You can focus on fulfilling God's purpose and "move toward fulfilling it without fear or anxiety because of His guaranteed 100 percent provision." Your job is to trust God and focus on doing His will. His job is to provide for you. Is anything keeping you from proceeding toward God's purposes for you? If so, how do Paul's words strengthen you to trust in the Lord?

God's Word Shows Us the Way

If you're unsure of where God wants you to focus your time and energies, Titus 2:3-5 is a perfect place to start. Which one or two of the ten essentials listed in your book need your attention right away? Note them here. Then focus on them. Prepare to tackle them, plan them into your schedule, and proceed ahead, praying all the way. And stand back and behold the provision of God!

Reflecting the Heart of Jesus

Read this final section in your book again. As you consider your character, jot down two or three changes or actions that would cause you to be more focused on God's purposes and better reflect the heart of Jesus.

~ A Prayer to Pray ~

What can you add to the prayer in your book that will more specifically describe your desire to be more focused?

Day 9

Forgiving

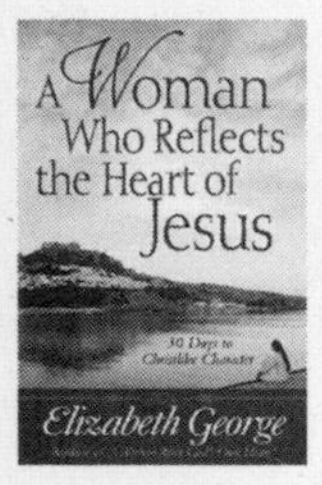

In your copy of *A Woman Who Reflects the Heart of Jesus*, read the chapter entitled "Forgiving." What encouraged you the most about your journey to Christlike character, and why?

What challenged you the most, and why?

Jesus Shows Us the Way

Sin began with man's disobedience to God, and forgiveness began with God forgiving the sinners. Scan Genesis 3:1-24. How did sin enter the world, and how did it affect Adam and Eve (verses 1-7)?

How did sin affect Adam and Eve's relationship with God, and with each other (verses 8-13)?

What were the consequences of sin for...

the serpent (verses 14-15)?

Eve (verse 16)?

Adam (verses 17-19,23-24)?

Adam and Eve (verses 23-24)?

In what ways do you see God's provision for and forgiveness of Adam and Eve for their sin (verse 21)?

Forgive That Your Father May Also Forgive You

Read Mark 11:25-26. What is one essential for prayer, and what is one very huge blessing that results to you personally when you take care of that one essential?

What instruction does 1 John 1:9 give for forgiveness?

Reflecting On Your Heart

"Forgiving others begins with God." Before you pray again, evaluate your relationship with God and with others. Are there others you need to forgive? Take time to reflect on your heart. Then do what needs to be done.

Love One Another

Jesus desired that we live in love, not hate. Read John 13:34-35. Exactly what does Jesus command of His followers, including you, and what standard or example does He set for us? And what is the outcome of doing as Jesus asks?

Do Good to Those Who Hate You

Everyone has "people problems." After reading Luke 6:27-31, note Jesus' three-step plan for nurturing a heart that loves and can readily forgive.

Step 1 (verse 27)—

Step 2 (verse 28)—

Step 3 (verse 28)—

Reflecting On Your Heart

In this section you read about activating and defrosting your own cold heart and willfully moving toward forgiving a person who has wronged you. Can you think of one act or step you need to take this week toward someone who has wronged or hurt you in some way? Make a plan, pray, and proceed on your plan. Your relationships with the Lord Jesus and the person you forgive will be improved!

Forgive Men Their Trespasses

You may have memorized the Lord's Prayer. It contains the basic elements of biblical prayer. Write out Matthew 6:12 here. What is assumed of you before you ask God for His forgiveness of your wrongs, sins, or trespasses?

How Often Shall I Forgive?

You'll love reading through Matthew 18:21-35. After you do, look again at verses 21-22.

What was Peter's question of Jesus?

And what was Jesus' answer?

In your own words, what was Jesus saying?

Father, Forgive Them

See Luke 23:26-46. Describe the scene, then explain what is happening in this passage.

Write out Jesus' prayer from the cross (verse 34). These dozen words have been heralded down through the centuries as the most amazing words ever spoken. They were the very reason Jesus was dying.

A question for your heart: Jesus prayed for the Father to forgive sinners. Yet to obtain salvation, His forgiveness needs to be accepted by sinners. Have you personalized God's forgiveness for your sins by receiving His Son as your Savior? If so, profuse thankfulness is the appropriate response. So is extending forgiveness to others. If not, John 1:12 and 3:16 can help guide you to Christ.

Reflecting the Heart of Jesus

Read this final section in your book again. As you consider your character, jot down two or three changes or actions that would cause you to be more forgiving of others and better reflect the heart of Jesus.

~ A Prayer to Pray ~

What can you add to the prayer in your book that will more specifically describe your desire to be more forgiving?

Day 10

Generous

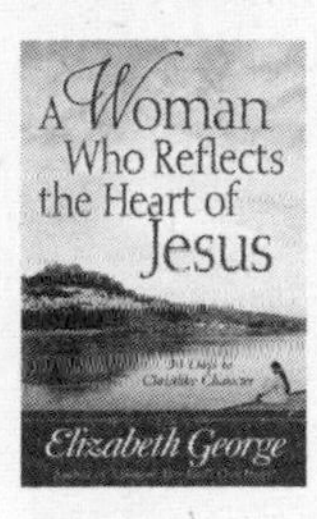

In your copy of *A Woman Who Reflects the Heart of Jesus*, read the chapter entitled "Generous." What encouraged you the most about your journey to Christlike character, and why?

What challenged you the most, and why?

Jesus Shows Us the Way

Perhaps the key verse of this chapter is Matthew 20:28. Read it in your Bible now in preparation for looking at the incredible generosity of our Lord. What have you already learned in general about generosity from reading this section in your book?

For Your Sake Jesus Became Poor

Read 2 Corinthians 8:7-15. Paul is writing to the church in Corinth to encourage the people to be more generous in their giving. In your own words, why is your giving important (verses 13-14)?

The Widow Gave All She Had

Read Mark 12:42-44. What distinguished this poor widow's offering from those of the others?

Reflecting On Your Heart

"Generosity has nothing to do with how much you have, but everything to do with how much you give in proportion to how much you have." What principle for your own giving can you draw from the heart of the widow in Mark 12:42-44, and how does her generous heart challenge you?

Where Your Treasure Is, There Your Heart Will Be

Now look at 2 Corinthians 9:6-8 and note the key truths about giving and generosity in...

verse 6—

verse 7—

What assurance does Paul give in verse 8 to keep you from worrying about your needs?

Reflecting On Your Heart

"Giving is...a matter of the heart. Giving is to be an act of worship." As you think about the blessing promised in verse 6 and the heart issues addressed in verses 7 and 8, what is keeping you from being more generous to God's causes and His people?

Do Good to Those Who Hate You

Read Matthew 5:44 and list the three steps for loving your enemies:

Step 1—

Step 2—

Step 3—

I'm sure you have people in your life who are not necessarily enemies, but they do make your life miserable. Read this section again and choose some ways you can be generous at heart toward these people.

Give to the Poor, and Follow Jesus

Read in Matthew 19:16-22 about the young man who came to Jesus asking about eternal life. How did this man ultimately demonstrate the priorities of his heart when the Lord asked him to sell all and follow Him (verse 22)?

Now read about Zacchaeus in Luke 19:1-9. What was Jesus' request, and how did Zacchaeus demonstrate his heart and priorities?

Reflecting On Your Heart

Are you feeling the need for a "priority makeover"? Dare to take a look at your bank statement from last month and your latest credit card statement. Jot down all indications of generosity to your church, to charitable organizations, and to people in need. Now compare that list with the rest of your expenditures. What does this reveal about your heart and priorities, and what will you do about your findings?

Lay Up for Yourselves Treasure in Heaven

Jesus urged us to store up our treasures in heaven. At the same time, what negative command did He give in Matthew 6:19-21, and why?

Can you share about a time when some "thing" you were saving, storing, or holding onto was ruined, lost, or stolen? Look at 1 Timothy 6:6-8 and write down the message in each verse that reveals God's perspective on your life and what's truly important.

Verse 6—

Verse 7—

Verse 8—

Did you have a "Wow!" moment that signaled changes you need to make in your heart and your perspective? Note the Number One change you need to make.

Reflecting the Heart of Jesus

Read this final section in your book again. As you consider your character, jot down two or three changes or actions that would cause you to be more generous to people and better reflect the heart of Jesus.

~ A Prayer to Pray ~

What can you add to the prayer in your book that will more specifically describe your desire to be more generous?

Day 11

Gentle

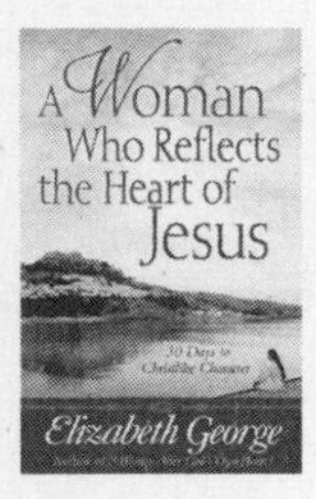

In your copy of *A Woman Who Reflects the Heart of Jesus*, read the chapter entitled "Gentle." What encouraged you the most about your journey to Christlike character, and why?

What challenged you the most, and why?

Jesus Shows Us the Way

Take My Yoke upon You

Read Matthew 11:28-30 again and describe the results of the religious yokes the people were forced to endure (verse 28).

What was Jesus' offer to these burdened people (verse 28)?

What was Jesus' double invitation to those who would follow Him (verse 29)?

—

—

What would make this yoke tolerable (verse 30)?

Jesus repeated this blessing: How would His yoke benefit those who chose to follow Him (verse 29)?

Reflecting On Your Heart

"Jesus offers relief as you exchange your methods of managing life for the ease that comes from yoking yourself with Jesus." Name several burdens you are shouldering today.

What is keeping you from exchanging your heavy burdens for His light and easy yoke?

Based on verses 28 and 29, what will happen when you make this transfer?

Your King Is Coming

Read Matthew 21:1-11. How would you compare the crowd's reaction with the present-day actions at a major sports event?

How did Jesus, the King, arrive into Jerusalem, and with what attitude (verse 5)?

Reflecting On Your Heart

"Make sure your times of worship...communicate your love and adoration for your Savior." As you enter into your times of worship at church or in private, are you reserved, preoccupied, dutiful, or exhilarated? Circle one and make a "note to self" regarding any changes of heart you need to make.

Others Show Us the Way

The world is a hostile place. The Bible contains many instances of violence. But, because God is love, Scripture also includes many instances and examples of men and women who were gentle even in a time of harshness. Let's notice a few now.

He Fell on His Face

See for yourself how Moses responded to the threats, accusations, and rebellion against him and his authority in the following verses.

In each instance, briefly note the problem, then write out how Moses displayed gentleness in his response.

Exodus 15:22-25—

Exodus 17:1-4—

Numbers 14:2-5—

Numbers 16:3-4—

What was God's testimony about Moses in Numbers 12:3?

How does 1 Peter 5:6 apply to Moses' actions and your attitudes today?

Let It Be to Me According to Your Word

In Luke 1:26-38, read about Mary's experience and her response to the angel who spoke to her. Explain the part gentleness played in Mary's acceptance of her new role.

Gentleness and Your Walk with Jesus

Look at the following scriptures in your Bible, and explain how gentleness applies to these issues:

Abundant living (Matthew 5:5)—

Confrontation (Proverbs 15:1 and 18)—

As a reflection of love (Ephesians 4:2)—

As a characteristic of a Christian (Colossians 3:12-13)—

Opposition (2 Timothy 2:24-25)—

Submission to God (James 1:21)—

Viewed by God in women (1 Peter 3:3-4)—

Check, circle, or star several truths that were new to you or good reminders of the meaning and importance of gentleness in your life. Jot down any that convicted your heart about needed change in your life.

Reflecting the Heart of Jesus

Read this final section in your book again. As you consider your character, jot down two or three changes or actions that would cause you to be more gentle and better reflect the heart of Jesus.

~ A Prayer to Pray ~

What can you add to the prayer in your book that will more specifically describe your desire to be more gentle?

Day 12

Good

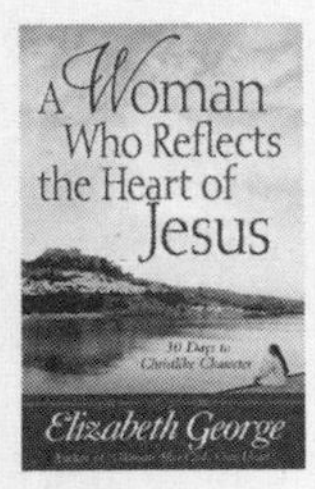

In your copy of *A Woman Who Reflects the Heart of Jesus*, read the chapter entitled "Good." What encouraged you the most about your journey to Christlike character, and why?

What challenged you the most, and why?

God Shows Us the Way

The Bible abounds with truths about God's goodness. Look in your Bible at the truths mentioned in this chapter of your book and summarize what you learn:

Exodus 33:19—

Exodus 34:6—

Romans 8:28—

How does knowing that God is only good and can only do good encourage you as you walk through your days?

Jesus Shows Us the Way

Good Teacher, What Good Thing Shall I Do?

Read the story of the rich young ruler in Matthew 19:16-22. This young man addressed Jesus as "good." Using a dictionary, write out the definition of good, and describe how Jesus fits this definition.

Explain how "good" works can never get a person to heaven, according to Matthew 5:48.

According to Romans 4:5, what is the only acceptable substitute for works, and what does it accomplish? Be sure and think about where you are placing your faith—in Christ's work on the cross, or in your good works.

Lord, Do You Want Us to Command Fire?

Describe the difference between the disciples' motives in Luke 9:51-56 and Jesus' motives in John 2:13-16.

Reflecting On Your Heart

"Every mean or cruel act done against you is an opportunity for you to reflect Jesus...and dispense God's goodness." How does this statement change your view of any mistreatment against you?

How do you generally respond to the unkind words and actions of others? And how does Jesus' example help you prepare for a better response the next time someone is hostile or unkind to you?

When You Do a Charitable Deed

Read Matthew 6:3-4. How secret should your good deeds be (verse 3)?

Who sees every good deed, whether done in public or privately, and what is the result (verse 4)?

Reflecting On Your Heart

"Keep your focus on the people you're helping, not on what you might gain for yourself." It's time for a heart checkup. What generally motivates your good deeds, and has anything in this lesson changed your heart? Can you think of any "secret deeds" you can do for someone this week?

Goodness and Good Works

See Galatians 5:22 in your Bible. Goodness is a fruit of the Spirit that you exhibit when you are walking in the Spirit (verse 16). What does Ephesians 5:8-10 say about how to grow in the quality of goodness?

Goodness moves into action and helps others, including other women. Read Titus 2:3-5 and comment on how these verses apply to goodness and to you...

as an older woman (not in age, but spiritual maturity)—

as a teacher to women—

as a wife, mother, homemaker—

Now read 1 Timothy 5:9-10. These verses describe the good services of widows and their eligibility to be cared for physically and financially by the church. How do their good works instruct and inspire your service in your church?

Read 1 Timothy 2:9-10 and comment on the focus of your Christian life and service as seen in...

verse 9—

verse 10—

You've looked at Titus 2:3-5 and God's desire that you help other women understand how they can be good and teach what is good. What are the instructions regarding good works...

to Titus (verse 7)?

to all of God's people (verse 14)?

Work at Doing What Is Good

Being good (or righteous) is what God provides to you through His Son, Jesus. And *doing* good is what results from your relationship with Jesus. Look again at the list of instructions from God about *doing* good. How are you doing? Note any commitments and changes you need to make.

Work at doing what is good.

Prove what is good.

Hold fast to what is good.

Overcome evil with good.

Strive to do what is good.

Follow after what is good.

Be zealous for what is good.

Reflecting the Heart of Jesus

Read this final section in your book again. As you consider your character, jot down two or three changes or actions that would cause you to display more goodness and better reflect the heart of Jesus.

~ A Prayer to Pray ~

What can you add to the prayer in your book that will more specifically describe your desire to do good?

Day 13

Gracious

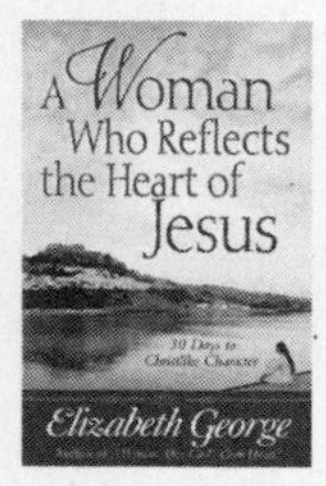

In your copy of *A Woman Who Reflects the Heart of Jesus*, read the chapter entitled "Gracious." What encouraged you the most about your journey to Christlike character, and why?

What challenged you the most, and why?

Jesus Shows Us the Way

Jesus possessed graciousness and conducted Himself with gracious behavior at all times. Note Jesus' consistently gracious spirit as He walked among His imperfect creation!

All Marveled at the Gracious Words

In Luke 4:1-13 we read that Jesus was tempted by the devil for 40 days and nights in the wilderness. In no way did Jesus emerge from this testing in weakness! What do we witness about Him instead in verse 14?

Now scan Luke 4:15-22. How did the power of the Holy Spirit affect His speech (verse 22)?

How does this power relate to your own gracious speech?

Reflecting On Your Heart

"The source of your speech is your own heart." What are the guidelines for your speech as outlined in Ephesians 4:29?

List several ways you can safeguard your heart so your words positively edify and encourage others.

You Are Troubled About Many Things

Enjoy reading about the two women in Luke 10:38-42. These two sisters, Mary and Martha, illustrate several qualities in this book. Here Martha shows not only the beauty of graciousness, but how ugly a lack of it is.

First, how did Martha show gracious hospitality (verse 38)?

Second, how did Martha show a lack of grace toward her sister (verse 40)?

And then toward Jesus (verse 40)?

Reflecting On Your Heart

"What is your patience level" with people? Take a peek at Titus 3:2 and search your heart...and your actions...and your words. Would you—and others—say you're like Martha with her ups and downs? What can you do to change this?

What Do You Want Me to Do for You?

Mercy is graciousness in action. Jesus had compassion, which prompted Him to graciously give two blind beggars their sight. Read Matthew 20:29-34. How did the crowd treat these men (verse 31)?

How did Jesus treat them (verses 32 and 34)?

Reflecting On Your Heart

Are you "walking among God's creation showing forth His grace mixed in with His compassion and mercy"? Are you "reflecting the great and gracious heart of Jesus"? It's a tall order, isn't it? But God's grace is sufficient to help you copy Jesus' character, including His graciousness.

Pray now to be more aware and sensitive to those who need Jesus' gracious "touch" through you.

Prepare to ask those in your daily path, "What do you want me to do for you?" Then...

Pause like Jesus did when you see a need. And...

Plan to open your heart and share the great and gracious heart of Jesus.

I Have Prayed for You

Prayer is a key avenue of extending God's grace. Look at Luke 22:31-32 to see Jesus modeling this. He didn't judge or give up on His disciple—He prayed for him. What would Peter soon face (verse 31)?

How did Jesus strengthen and encourage Peter (verse 32)?

Who do you know who is struggling in faith, facing health issues, or discouraged? Write down a few names...and pray!

Reflecting On Your Heart

"How do you act (or react!) when someone lets you down?" I'm sure like Jesus, you know people who have failed you. Now is your chance to act like Jesus. How can you be gracious? Are you praying for them? Are you looking at their potential? Are you trying to understand their struggles? What encouragement can you give?

The Proverbs 31 Woman Shows Us the Way

Treat yourself and read the complete passage on the magnificent and gracious woman in Proverbs 31:10-31. Write down the character qualities featured in these verses:

Verse 20—

How will you reach out to the poor and needy?

Verse 25—

How would you wear these qualities in a room full of people?

Verse 26—

What changes do you need to make in your speech?

Verse 30—

What is the key to her many gracious character qualities?

Reflecting the Heart of Jesus

Read this final section in your book again. As you consider your character, jot down two or three changes or actions that would cause you to display a more gracious attitude and better reflect the heart of Jesus.

~ A Prayer to Pray ~

What can you add to the prayer in your book that will more specifically describe your desire to be more gracious?

Day 14

Humble

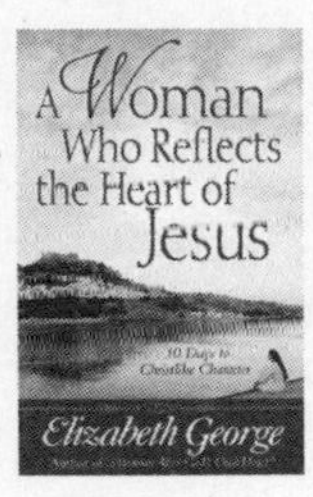

In your copy of *A Woman Who Reflects the Heart of Jesus*, read the chapter entitled "Humble." What encouraged you the most about your journey to Christlike character, and why?

What challenged you the most, and why?

Jesus Shows Us the Way

To begin, read Philippians 2:5-8. Here the apostle Paul describes how Jesus shows us the way to humility.

If you wish to follow in the steps of Jesus, you must remember that the way up is down. Pick out several of the "downward" steps Jesus took in His humility (verses 6-8).

On a human level, what was the result of Jesus' humiliation (verse 8)?

Now look at the command Paul states in verse 5, and list several immediate thoughts about how you can obey it.

I Must Decrease

How popular had John the Baptist become, according to Matthew 3:5-6?

Read John 1:23-27. When asked to identify himself, what was John's very humble description of himself (verse 23)?

Write out John's final statement regarding himself in verse 27.

What does John teach you about humility?

Reflecting On Your Heart

Read Philippians 2:1-4 and note the "how tos" for humility in...

verse 3—

verse 4—

After seeing the humility of Jesus in verses 5-8 and observing the steps toward humility in verses 3 and 4, list two or three changes that must take place in your thinking and actions so you are more like Jesus.

Blessed Are the Peacemakers

Take a look at Philippians 4:2-3. What was Paul's desire for the two women mentioned here (verse 2)?

Jesus lived and taught the concept of peace among Christians. What famous statement did He make—and live by—in Matthew 5:9?

Now think about the squabble between the two women in Philippians 4:2-3, Euodia and Syntyche. Are you the source of any contention in your home or family, your church, your circle of friends? If so, what do you plan to do to stop it and to begin reflecting Jesus' humility in each of those places?

Reflecting On Your Heart

"Your calling is to keep your eyes on Jesus, not on those around you." When you humbly do your job, what will be the fruit of your ministry?

Whoever Humbles Himself Will Be Exalted

Quickly look up the following verses and write out the key message regarding humility that reminds us "whoever humbles himself will be exalted":

Matthew 23:11—

Luke 13:30—

Luke 14:7-10—

Luke 17:33—

Luke 18:14—

Based on what you are learning about humility, how should you behave the next time you are at church or a shower, wedding, party, or potluck?

The Lord Looks at the Heart

Read 1 Samuel 16:7 and write out the final sentence.

Now read Luke 18:10-14 in your Bible. After observing the two men, what did Jesus say about humility in verse 14?

A key passage on humility is 1 Peter 5:5-6. Again, read it in your Bible and write out the commands and God's blessings for obeying them:

	God's Command	*God's Blessing*
Verse 5—		
Verse 6—		

In preparation for the next section—and to witness a powerful example of humility—read John 13:1-5. Summarize in a sentence or two what you learn about "The Order of the Towel."

I Have Given You an Example

Quickly scan John 13:6-15. In verse 15, what did Jesus tell His disciples to do, and why?

Sometimes we think certain acts are beneath us—or we don't think at all! As a woman who desires to reflect the heart of Jesus, how does His example of humble service move you to pay attention to the needs of others and gladly do what needs to be done?

Reflecting the Heart of Jesus

Read this final section in your book again. As you consider your character, jot down two or three changes or actions that would cause you to be more humble and better reflect the heart of Jesus.

~ A Prayer to Pray ~

What can you add to the prayer in your book that will more specifically describe your desire to be more humble?

Day 15

Joyful

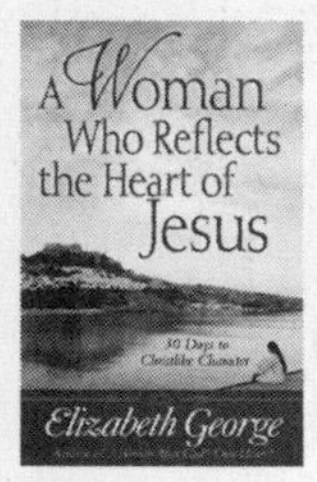

In your copy of *A Woman Who Reflects the Heart of Jesus*, read the chapter entitled "Joyful." What encouraged you the most about your journey to Christlike character, and why?

What challenged you the most, and why?

Jesus Shows Us the Way

Take a look at Isaiah 61:10 in your Bible. Then stop and do as Isaiah did: "greatly rejoice in the LORD" and the salvation and righteousness He has given to you.

Briefly explain the difference between the "happiness" the world knows and true spiritual joy.

Joy No Matter What

According to John 15:10-11, what was the basis of Jesus' joy?

What does Jesus say is the basis for your joy?

Here's a thought question: If obedience is the basis for your joy, then what will determine the level or depth of your joy?

How's your joy? Or maybe a better question is, How's your obedience? Check your heart and make plans for improved obedience...and joy!

No One Will Take Your Joy from You

Begin by reading John 16:21-22. Here, Jesus spoke to His disciples about sorrow and joy. What real-life happening does Jesus use as an illustration of sorrow in verse 21?

On the heels of the bad news, Jesus shares the good news. How did He comfort His disciples in verse 22?

How do you tend to handle the disappointments and sufferings of daily life? Do you let them get you down? Do you sink into a depression or get angry? Jot down the wrong responses you give most frequently during trials.

Now for the really good news! What assurance, promise, and truth do you read in the final statement in verse 22?

Ask...That Your Joy May Be Full

According to John 16:24, how does prayer give you joy?

Jesus said to His disciples, "Until now you have asked nothing in My name." Are you asking? If not, what will you do about Jesus' command to "ask"?

Reflecting On Your Heart

"Stay close to Jesus and He will keep you on an even keel, no matter how overwhelming or devastating your circumstances." Prayer is a matter of the heart. Are you praying? Are you faithfully looking up when your heart is burdened? You can have joy when you choose to pray—when you, like Isaiah, determine "I will rejoice in the Lord." What choices are you making?

The Joy That Was Set Before Jesus

Look reverently at Hebrews 12:2 and the joy Jesus experienced while facing and enduring His death on the cross. What does this verse say you are to do to experience joy in your difficult circumstances?

Reflecting On Your Heart

The "joy that Jesus experienced in His darkest hour is also available to you." How are you presently facing your hard times? Make notes below. Are your eyes and heart fixed on Jesus? If not, do as Hebrews 12:2 tells you: look to Jesus.

Hannah Shows Us the Way

Briefly scan Hannah's story in 1 Samuel 1:1-18. What made her life so miserable (verses 1-7)?

How is her sorrow described in verse 10?

What was Hannah's solution to her agony (see verses 10 and 12) and the end result (verses 17-18)?

Bonus question: Hannah truly shows us the way to joy. Scan Hannah's song of praise and prophecy in 1 Samuel 2:1-10. In one word, what do you see as the primary focus of Hannah's utter joy in these verses?

God's Word Shows Us the Way

Read again about the changes you can make to ensure you experience joy throughout your life, no matter what. Which one or ones can give you immediate help for the problems you face now?

Reflecting the Heart of Jesus

Read this final section in your book again. As you consider your character, jot down two or three changes or actions that would cause you to be more joyful and better reflect the heart of Jesus.

~ A Prayer to Pray ~

What can you add to the prayer in your book that will more specifically describe your desire to be more joyful?

Day 16

Kind

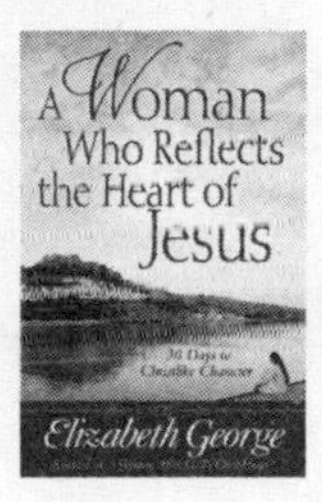

In your copy of *A Woman Who Reflects the Heart of Jesus*, read the chapter entitled "Kind." What encouraged you the most about your journey to Christlike character, and why?

What challenged you the most, and why?

God Shows Us the Way

The initially unkind prophet Jonah knew about God's attribute of kindness. Read Jonah 4:2 in your Bible and list the many qualities Jonah credited to God.

Again in your Bible, see how Paul described God in Ephesians 2:7. How does he refer to God's greatest act of kindness?

Reflecting On Your Heart

This book is all about reflecting God's character. Considering that "God's great heart is a heart filled and overflowing with kindness" and all He has done for you, how can you extend His kindness to others? Please be specific.

Jesus Shows Us the Way

Before you begin, according to the information in your book, what is the difference between *kind* and *nice*?

What Great Things the Lord Has Done for You

Mark 5:3-5 is quoted in your book, but quickly read through verses 1-20 in your Bible. How did the people respond to Jesus' act of kindness in verse 17?

How did the man who had been possessed by demons respond to Jesus' act of kindness in verse 18?

What were Jesus' instructions to this man (verse 19)?

Bonus question: What words did Mary, the mother of Jesus, use while praising God in Luke 1:49?

Reflecting On Your Heart

In the space below or on another page write out a short testimonial of some of the "great things the Lord has done for you." Be sure to share it with someone who doesn't know the great and kind God you serve. Your testimony is meant to be shared.

Go and Sin No More

Scan John 8:1-11 and, in your own words, describe how Jesus showed kindness to a sinner without condoning her sin.

Based on Jesus' words to this woman, how can you best honor Jesus' sacrifice for sin as you live out your life?

He Put His Hands on His Eyes

Jesus was very personable. He was not afraid to be with people or to touch them. As you read Mark 8:22-26, make a list of the evidence that points to the amount of time, attention, and care our Lord extended to this needy man.

Scripture gives many other examples of Jesus' kindness. Describe a few of these examples of Jesus touching those who suffered.

	Problem	*Jesus' Solution*
Matthew 8:3		
Matthew 8:15		
Matthew 9:27-30		
Matthew 20:29-34		
Mark 7:25-30		
Luke 7:12-15		

He Took Them Up in His Arms

Picture Jesus' act of kindness as you read Mark 10:13-16. How was His treatment of the folks who gathered different from the disciples'?

Reflecting On Your Heart

"Jesus loved, welcomed, enjoyed, and blessed the children." How should His example of tenderhearted kindness affect the way you respond to your family? To all children? To others?

Kindness can melt the coldest of hearts. Try warming up someone's cold heart today with an act of kindness. Do you know who it might be? And what you could do for that person? Formulate a plan below. Then go and reflect Jesus!

Women in the Bible Show Us the Way

He Can Turn in Here

Briefly describe how the Shunammite woman showed kindness to Elisha in 2 Kings 4:8-10.

How does her kindness and hospitality speak to you?

Abounding with Deeds of Kindness

Now enjoy reading about another great lady, Dorcas, in Acts 9:36-41. How was her kindness displayed, and to whom?

How did Dorcas live out the definition of true religion found in James 1:27?

Be Kind to One Another

Kindness is a fruit of the Spirit. Therefore, according to the following verses, what must take place in order for you to exhibit kindness in your life?

The command (Galatians 5:16)—

The caution (Ephesians 4:30-32)—

Reflecting the Heart of Jesus

Read this final section in your book again. As you consider your character, jot down two or three changes or actions that would cause you to be more kind and better reflect the heart of Jesus.

~ A Prayer to Pray ~

What can you add to the prayer in your book that will more specifically describe your desire to be more kind?

Day 17

Loving

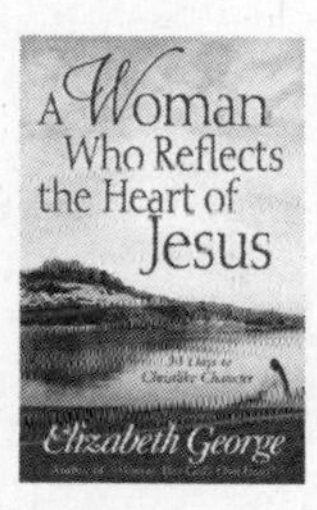

In your copy of *A Woman Who Reflects the Heart of Jesus*, read the chapter entitled "Loving." What encouraged you the most about your journey to Christlike character, and why?

What challenged you the most, and why?

God Shows Us Love

After reading through the list of verses provided in your book that describe God's love, pick one that has special meaning to you and share why. (A good bonus exercise is to look up each verse in your Bible.)

Jesus Shows Us the Way

Jesus' Teachings on Love

Again, as with God's love, read through the list of verses provided in your book on Jesus' teachings about love. Pick one that has special meaning to you and share why. (Once again, an excellent bonus exercise is to look up each verse in your Bible.)

Jesus' Practice of Love

Jesus loved His friends—What do you learn from the following verses about Jesus' friendship with three siblings?

Luke 10:38-39—

John 11:1-5—

John 12:1-3—

Reflecting On Your Heart

"The mark of a true friend is persistent love, regardless of any burdens the friendship presents." Look at Proverbs 18:24 and note what it says about a good friend. Think about your own relationships. What proof can you offer that you are this kind of loving friend to your friends?

Jesus loved His fellow-workers—Look up John 13:1. What impresses you most about Jesus' love for His own, His disciples?

Selfishness and laziness are culprits to not living and showing love. How can you turn up the dedication of your love for your own—your family and best friends?

Reflecting On Your Heart

"Remember Jesus." Love is a matter of the heart. Can you think of a good friend or family member toward whom your love is slipping or cooling off? What changes can you make to show active love and once again reflect the heart of Jesus?

Jesus loved the lost—It is worthwhile to look at all three descriptions of the rich young ruler's encounter with Jesus. Begin by reading Mark 10:17-22. Then below, write any additional facts found in the other two versions of this account:

Matthew 19:16-22—

Luke 18:18-23—

What insights did you discover from Jesus' interactions with this man for your encounters with the lost?

Reflecting On Your Heart

How's your heart for the lost? Do you pray for them? Do you love them like Jesus did? How does the statement, "They aren't the enemy, only victims of the enemy" affect your perception of non-Christians you come in contact with on a daily basis?

Jesus' Love Was Sacrificial

How did God the Father show His love, according to John 3:16?

Read Romans 5:8. How did the Son of God, Jesus Christ, show His love?

There is a lot of information about God's sacrificial love in this one paragraph in your book. Now let's take it apart. Write your answers from the paragraph.

How does love begin?

How is the power to love gained?

What serves as evidence that your love is growing?

What command does God give in 1 John 4:21?

What is the one thing you are *not* to love, according to 1 John 2:15?

What else are you not to love, according to 1 Timothy 6:10?

Now that you've been through this list of the ways and means of sacrificial love, check the one that needs your immediate prayer and attention. Jot down a brief plan for polishing up this most excellent and basic character quality of a woman who loves God.

Reflecting the Heart of Jesus

Read this final section in your book again. As you consider your character, jot down two or three changes or actions that would cause you to be more loving to people and better reflect the heart of Jesus.

~ A Prayer to Pray ~

What can you add to the prayer in your book that will more specifically describe your desire to be more loving?

Day 18

Patient

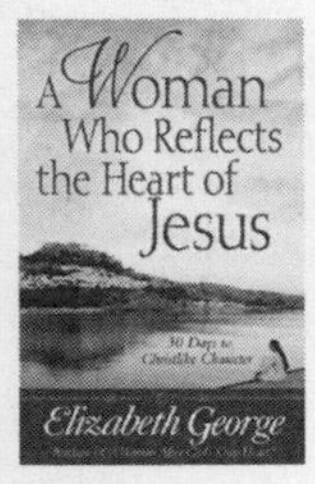

In your copy of *A Woman Who Reflects the Heart of Jesus*, read the chapter entitled "Patient." What encouraged you the most about your journey to Christlike character, and why?

What challenged you the most, and why?

Jesus Shows Us the Way

Don't you yearn to have the grace to endure trying circumstances with an even disposition? That's patience! And don't you want to be known by others as a woman who doesn't complain, doesn't murmur, doesn't protest? That's patience! Patience is a divine characteristic. Look at 1 Peter 3:20. How did the apostle Peter explain this divine quality as seen in God the Father?

Patience is like a diamond—there are many facets to this single character quality Jesus possessed, and that you and I need, too. Follow along as Jesus teaches about patience.

How Often Shall I Forgive?

On a scale of 1 to 10, how would you rate your patience level in the scenarios described below—with 1 meaning you have no patience, and 10 meaning you are totally patient?

When you are wronged once—

When you are wronged repeatedly—

Peter asked Jesus a question about the extent to which we should show patience. Read about it now in Matthew 18:21-23. How did Jesus answer Peter's question?

Look at Colossians 3:12-13. Because patience is a characteristic of the "new man," how should it affect your forgiveness of others according to verse 13?

How does Galatians 6:1 add to your understanding of the patience required in forgiving others?

Can you think of two or three ways you can raise the level of your patience and forgiveness of others?

A Right Response to Abuse

Read the details of one portion of Jesus' trial in Matthew 26:57-68. What occurred that caused Jesus to break His silence (verse 63)?

What was the nature of the high priest's oath, and how did Jesus reply (verses 63 and 64)?

Read 1 Peter 2:21-23. Jesus did speak up. However, what characterized His words even when He was under great pressure (verse 23)?

Instead of lashing out, what did Jesus do (verse 23)?

What do you learn from Jesus about handling tense situations?

Reflecting On Your Heart

"Looking to God through prayer is always the best response to any difficult situation." Can you give several reasons that prayer is such an important element in living out patience in an imperfect and impatient world?

Love Your Enemies

You *must* read Luke 6:27-28 in your Bible—or even consider memorizing it! Loving your enemies starts with prayer as you single out those who have hurt or persecuted you. Patience is exercised as you leave these problem people in the hands of God. List a few people (first names or initials only!) who you might classify as your enemies. Then ask God to help you decide how you can show love and kindness to them. Of course you can pray, but how can you go beyond prayer and love them through kind words and actions? List three things you can do to show love to your enemies.

—

—

—

But One Thing Is Needed

Impatience is never a good thing, especially when it's shown toward your family...and definitely when it's shown toward the Lord! How did Martha fail on all counts as described in Luke 10:38-42? Write down everything she did that evidenced her lack of patience.

What did Jesus say would cure Martha's impatience (verses 41-42)?

Reflecting On Your Heart

"Jesus is telling you, as He told Martha, to refocus on what's really important: your relationship with Him." Now consider Mary. What was she doing that indicated her patient spirit, and how does she show you the importance of taking care of the one thing needed—putting first things first?

The Judge Is Standing at the Door!

Begin by reading James 5:7-9. What does verse 7 say about the Lord?

What does verse 9 say about the Judge?

God is doing His part. What does He ask of you in verses 7 and 8?

Reflecting On Your Heart

"In patience...wait on the Lord, wait for the Judge!" How are you at waiting—waiting on God, waiting on the Lord, waiting on the Judge? If you are in the "needs improvement" category, what are your plans for improvement?

Walk in the Spirit

How do these verses apply to your ability to patiently live for Jesus?

John 14:15-17—

Galatians 5:16 and 22—

Now read 1 Thessalonians 5:14. How do you positively contribute to the body of Christ when you are walking in the Spirit?

Reflecting the Heart of Jesus

Read this final section in your book again. As you consider your character, jot down two or three changes or actions that would cause you to be more patient with people and life situations, and better reflect the heart of Jesus.

~ A Prayer to Pray ~

What can you add to the prayer in your book that will more specifically describe your desire to be more patient?

Day 19

Peaceful

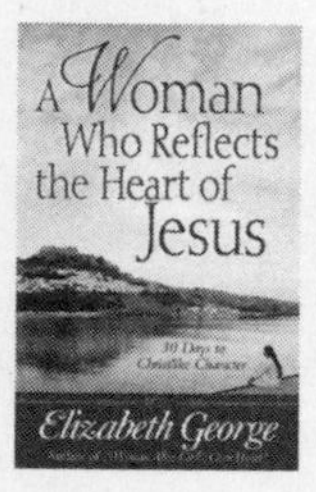

In your copy of *A Woman Who Reflects the Heart of Jesus*, read the chapter entitled "Peaceful." What encouraged you the most about your journey to Christlike character, and why?

What challenged you the most, and why?

In your book, read again through the truths about the attitude of peace.

Our peace has nothing to do with our situation...

Our peace has nothing to do with daily issues...

Our peace has nothing to do with what we have....

Our peace is an inward attitude...

Which truth about peace spoke the loudest to your heart, and why?

Jesus Shows Us the Way

Jesus' Example of Peace

Read in your Bible about Jesus' struggles in the garden of Gethsemane in Mark 14:33-42. What do you learn from Jesus about maintaining an attitude of peace in spite of your circumstances?

Reflecting On Your Heart

"You can either choose to give in to feelings of panic or dread, or you can place your trust in Him and be filled with His peace." In general, which reaction best describes your heart and your choices when you face difficult and trying situations? Then read on to discover more about peace.

Jesus Offers You His Peace

The Place of Peace—According to John 14:1-3, what kind of place is Jesus preparing for you and His people?

The Person of Peace—Continue onward and read verses 16-27. List at least five things or activities that describe the ministry of the Holy Spirit to you and other believers.

—

—

—

—

—

The Promise of Peace—Describe Jesus' contribution to the peace He promises you in...

Romans 5:1—

Philippians 4:7—

Reflecting On Your Heart

"In reality, only one thing—or Person—can offer you peace...It's Jesus." Is your heart caught up in distractions, escapism, amusements, hobbies, or travel as you seek the much-needed quality of peace? Why is Jesus the only source of true peace? Jot down the "things to do to get peace" found in Philippians 4:6 and 7.

What added word of encouragement does Philippians 4:9 give regarding peace?

Reflecting the Heart of Jesus

Read this final section in your book again. As you consider your character, jot down two or three changes or actions that would cause you to experience more peace of heart and mind and better reflect the heart of Jesus.

~ A Prayer to Pray ~

What can you add to the prayer in your book that will more specifically describe your desire to know more peace?

Day 20

Prayerful

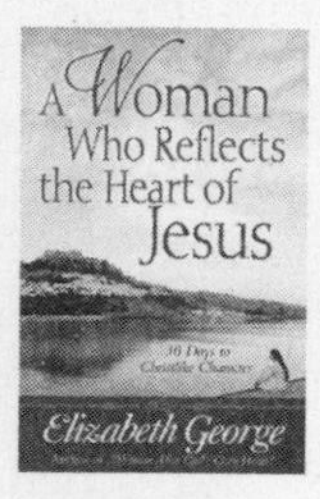

In your copy of *A Woman Who Reflects the Heart of Jesus*, read the chapter entitled "Prayerful." What encouraged you the most about your journey to Christlike character, and why?

What challenged you the most, and why?

Jesus Shows Us the Way

Pray for God's Will

Jesus made a habit of taking time to pray prior to important decisions or events. You are in for a treat as you view Him at prayer in the instances that follow.

Jesus prayed as He began His ministry—Read Luke 3:21-22 and 4:1. Describe what occurred as Jesus was praying, and what happened immediately afterward.

Now read Acts 4:31. What happened as the disciples prayed?

Describe the Holy Spirit's ongoing ministry as defined in...

1 Corinthians 12:7—

1 Corinthians 12:11—

1 Corinthians 12:18—

Jesus prayed as He chose His disciples—In your Bible, read Luke 6:12 and 13. Before Jesus selected His disciples, where did He pray, and for how long (verse 12)?

What does Jesus' example show you about the seriousness of making decisions?

Describe Jesus' prayer practices as witnessed in the following verses:

Mark 1:35—

Luke 5:15-16—

Luke 6:12—

Luke 9:18—

Luke 9:28—

Reflecting On Your Heart

"Like Jesus, pray." It's obvious Jesus was convinced prayer was vitally important when decisions had to be made and people were involved. What major decisions or events are coming up in your life that should compel you to seek God's guidance? List some here, and pray faithfully until God's direction is clear.

Jesus prayed before going to the cross—We can never read of Jesus praying in the garden without being moved...and instructed. What prayer principles do you learn from Jesus' time of prayer described in Matthew 26:36-46? (For your information, there are quite a few! Enjoy finding as many as possible.)

Reflecting On Your Heart

"God has given you an effective resource in prayer." Jesus prayed before facing death on a cross. What strength and guidance do you need for your future? List it here and begin to pray faithfully like Jesus did—fervently, frequently, all night if you need to.

Pray for One Another

Read John 17 and note a few specifics about how Jesus prayed for the "one anothers" in His life:

Who did He pray for in verses 1-5, and what did He ask?

Who did He pray for in verses 6-19, and what did He ask?

Who did He pray for in verses 20-26, and what did He ask?

Describe Jesus' present ministry to you and all believers as recorded in Hebrews 7:25.

Reflecting On Your Heart

"To reflect Jesus' heart for prayer, follow His example and pray for others." Make a list of at least three people who need prayer support. When will you pray for them?

Pray to Your Father

Read Matthew 6:5-6 to understand why God is to be the audience for all your prayers.

Make a list of the ugly actions and motives of the hypocrites (verse 5).

Make a list of God's instructions to you about your actions and motives for prayer (verse 6).

Lord, Teach Us to Pray

Read Jesus' model prayer in Matthew 6:9-13. Write out the six petitions. Notice that the first three are directed to God, and the second three speak to human needs.

Petition #1 (verse 9)—

Petition #2 (verse 10)—

Petition #3 (verse 10)—

Petition #4 (verse 11)—

Petition #5 (verse 12)—

Petition #6 (verse 13)—

As you look over this model prayer and balanced list, do you notice anything that's missing from the content of your prayers? Note it here, and purpose to incorporate it into your future prayers.

Reflecting the Heart of Jesus

Read this final section in your book again. As you consider your character, jot down two or three changes or actions that would cause you to be more prayerful and better reflect the heart of Jesus.

~ A Prayer to Pray ~

What can you add to the prayer in your book that will more specifically describe your desire to be more prayerful?

Day 21

Pure

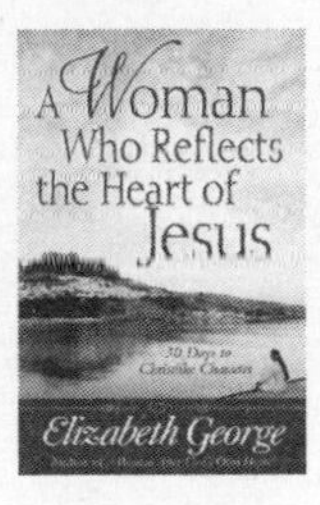

In your copy of *A Woman Who Reflects the Heart of Jesus*, read the chapter entitled "Pure." What encouraged you the most about your journey to Christlike character, and why?

What challenged you the most, and why?

The Holiness and Purity of God

God declares His holiness, or absolute purity, over 50 times in the book of Leviticus. Write out two examples here:

Leviticus 20:26—

Leviticus 22:32—

In Matthew 5:48, Jesus rephrases the standard set in Leviticus 19:2. Write it out here:

Believers Are Called to Be Like God

Throughout the book of Leviticus there is a continual emphasis on personal purity and holiness in response to God's holiness. Write out the following examples here:

Leviticus 11:45—

Leviticus 20:7—

According to Colossians 1:21-22, what made it possible for a believer to conform to this standard of pure holiness?

Look at Romans 12:1. Jesus has done His part. Now, what is your part in this process of being pure?

Jesus Shows Us the Way

Depart from Me, for I Am a Sinful Man

Peter recognized Jesus' unique pure and holy nature and responded in shame and remorse. Record how two others responded in awe to the resurrected Jesus.

Paul in Acts 9:3-4—

John in Revelation 1:17—

As a Christian, the Spirit of holiness is living in you. How are you responding to His presence, especially when you consider your sinfulness? When you think of Peter, Paul, and John's dramatic responses to Jesus' holy presence, do you think you should be more acutely aware—and careful—of your sin? Take a few minutes to reflect and respond.

How does 1 Corinthians 6:19 shake you up?

Reflecting On Your Heart

"Your purity begins when you recognize your sinfulness as well as Jesus' sinlessness and holiness." As you take this journey toward a more Christlike life, how is your awareness of your sinfulness changing in light of the purity of Jesus and the purity He desires of you?

This Man Has Done Nothing Wrong

Three people who came into contact with Jesus shortly before His crucifixion recognized His purity. Read these scriptures in your Bible and indicate how each of them responded.

Judas in Matthew 27:4—

Pilate's wife in Matthew 27:19—

The thief on the cross in Luke 23:41-43—

How are you responding to Jesus?

Truly This Was the Son of God!

Read Matthew 27:54. What was the conclusive response of the Roman soldiers involved in Jesus' execution as they observed Jesus and the surrounding events?

Reflecting On Your Heart

Purity is not optional for those who follow Jesus. It is commanded and expected of those who belong to Jesus and represent Him to others. To reflect His purity, you must strive to be pure in thought, word, and deed. Think of two or three immediate changes that would make you more Christlike. Then "thank Jesus for His sacrifice. And purpose to live in purity."

Understanding More About Purity

Purity is high on God's list of priorities for women—Titus 2:3-5 is God's checklist for you and your character. Read it again in your Bible, realizing that He calls you to be *pure, pure-minded,* and *chaste.* What effect should knowing God wants you to be pure have on you?

Purity doesn't just happen—Are you looking for ideas about what to do to be more like Jesus in regard to purity? Read 2 Timothy 2:22 and write out the two steps given there:

—

—

Purity comes from God's Word—According to Hebrews 4:12, God's Word can help you fight the battle for purity. In what ways can it help?

What steps are you taking to follow the advice of Psalm 119:11?

Purity comes from confession—What does 1 John 1:8-10 tell you about sin?

Verse 8—

Verse 9—

Verse 10—

Confession is a moment-by-moment activity. Are there issues you need to discuss and confess to the Lord? Rush to the Lord and talk to Him...now! Your purity is in jeopardy!

Reflecting the Heart of Jesus

Read this final section in your book again. As you consider your character, jot down two or three changes or actions that would help you in your ongoing battle for purity and your desire to better reflect the heart of Jesus.

~ A Prayer to Pray ~

What can you add to the prayer in your book that will more specifically describe your desire to be pure?

Day 22

Responsible

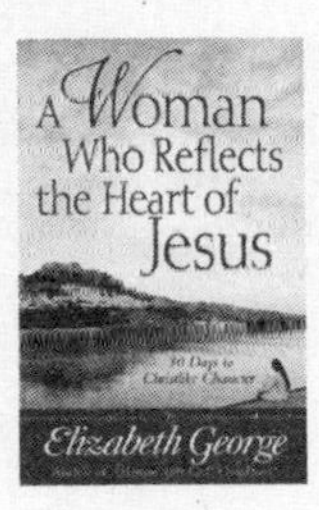

In your copy of *A Woman Who Reflects the Heart of Jesus*, read the chapter entitled "Responsible." What encouraged you the most about your journey to Christlike character, and why?

What challenged you the most, and why?

Jesus Shows Us the Way

To begin your study about being responsible, look up the word *responsible* in a dictionary and jot down several of its meanings.

None of Them Is Lost

For two staggering examples of Jesus' quality of responsibility, take notes on how He fulfilled His duty regarding you and your salvation...and how He will continue to do so.

John 17:12—

John 10:28—

How does knowing you can count on Jesus give you assurance?

Reflecting On Your Heart

Jesus cannot lie—period. When He promises you something, He is responsible to see it through. In a word or two, what does He promise you in the following verses?

Matthew 11:28-29

Matthew 16:18

John 14:1-3

John 15:26

John 16:33

Acts 1:8

He Appointed Twelve

After reading Mark 3:13-14, note Jesus' twofold purpose in choosing the 12 disciples.

—

—

In the end, these men would take Jesus' place after His death and carry out His ministry. What does this indicate about Jesus' responsibility?

What does this indicate about the disciples' responsibility?

Now it's your turn. As one who is to reflect Jesus, what is your responsibility?

Reflecting On Your Heart

"What do you have that's worthy of being passed on to others?" Jesus calls you to be responsible in the following ways:

To the world, Titus 2:5 says you are responsible to live in a way that ____________________.

To the next generation of women, Titus 2:3 says you are responsible to ______________ (verse 3) and ______________ (verse 4).

To your children of all ages, Titus 2:4 says you are responsible to ______________ them.

To your husband, Titus 2:4-5 says you are responsible to ______________ him.

For your character development, Titus 2:3 says you are responsible to be

____

____

____

He Will Give You Another Helper

The body of Christ is made up of those who help and those who are helped. You have been given spiritual gifts for the good of other believers. Read and pray over the lists in Romans 12:7-8 and 1 Corinthians 12:8-10. A first step to discovering and developing your spiritual gifts is to ask and answer, "If I could do anything in ministry that is indicated in these lists, what would it be?" Share it here...and pray!

Reflecting On Your Heart

"When you have more tasks than time or energy, look up. The Holy Spirit will give you 'the fruit of the Spirit'" to help you fulfill your responsibilities. Jesus has given you the Holy Spirit—a "Helper" in the spiritual realm. What responsibilities are you in charge of today?

First list them on your to-do list.

Next commit them to God in prayer.

Then walk in the Spirit through your day and your work.

Bonus item: Make a list of the fruit of the Spirit found in Galatians 5:22-23. Then proceed through your day exhibiting these qualities of Jesus.

Render to Caesar the Things That Are Caesar's

To see this responsibility mentioned in your Bible, look up Mark 12:13-17. What does Romans 13:1 add to the subject of being responsible to the government?

In what situation is there an exception to these teachings, according to Acts 4:18-20?

Reflecting On Your Heart

"As a citizen of both the kingdom of God and your nation, you are responsible to both God and your government." What are some ways you can demonstrate to your family and others that Christians have a responsibility to the government?

Guidelines for Responsibility

Be responsible—read each of the scriptures in your Bible. Then move through the guidelines for responsibly living out the will of God. Give a short statement regarding your desires to follow through on each guideline.

A responsible Christian is informed (2 Timothy 2:15)—

A responsible Christian is obedient (1 Peter 1:14-16)—

A responsible Christian is growing in faith (2 Peter 3:18)—

A responsible Christian uses her spiritual gifts (1 Corinthians 12:7)—

Reflecting the Heart of Jesus

Read this final section in your book again. As you consider your character, jot down two or three changes or actions that would cause you to be more responsible and better reflect the heart of Jesus.

~ A Prayer to Pray ~

What can you add to the prayer in your book that will more specifically describe your desire to be more responsible?

Day 23

Sensitive

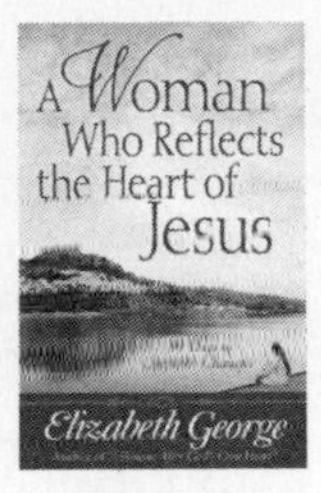

In your copy of *A Woman Who Reflects the Heart of Jesus*, read the chapter entitled "Sensitive." What encouraged you the most about your journey to Christlike character, and why?

What challenged you the most, and why?

Jesus Shows Us the Way

Jot down several dictionary definitions of the word *sensitivity*.

Look at the table of contents at the front of this book and list the other qualities you are studying in this volume that would benefit from the quality of sensitivity.

He Healed the Sick

Read Mark 1:21-34. Briefly describe what took place in verses 21-28.

Describe how Jesus was sensitive in...

verses 29-31—

verses 32-34—

Reflecting On Your Heart

A heart in tune with God is a heart in tune with those who are suffering. Are your heartstrings in tune with the Lord? Whether it was one ailing woman or the many people who were sick and demon-possessed, Jesus was sensitive to each need. "Pray for God to increase the range on your radar and your compassion level for others."

He Had Compassion on the Hurting

Read the story Jesus told of the Good Samaritan in Luke 10:30-37, and describe the responses of the three different people who came upon the person who was hurting.

The priest (verse 31)—

The Levite (verse 32)—

The Samaritan (verses 33-35)—

What lessons, both positive and negative, do you learn for yourself and for dealing with those who are hurting?

Reflecting On Your Heart

Sensitivity begins with noticing. But the next step is to ask, "How can I help?" What can you do today for someone you know is hurting?

He Will Not Cast Out Those Who Come to Him

Scan through John 4:1-26. Briefly note what you learn about reaching across all barriers in order to be sensitive to the needs of others.

He Cared for the Disabled

Note the prophecy contained in Luke 4:18 regarding the Messiah's ministry.

How do you see this fulfilled in the touching scene described in John 5:1-9?

How does Jesus' care for the disabled speak to your heart and maybe even your wallet?

He Loved the Unlovely

Ministering to the unlovely doesn't just happen. You have to be "out there" among the people—like Jesus was. Meet a despised man who *really* wanted to see Jesus. Read Luke 19:1-10 and describe the trouble Zacchaeus went through to catch a glimpse of Jesus, never dreaming he would actually get to talk with the Lord.

How did Jesus go above and beyond to reach out to Zacchaeus, and how did Zacchaeus respond to Jesus' sensitivity?

He Was Spiritually Sensitive

Jesus tended to the physical needs of others, yet His sensitivity went beyond the physical to include ministering to their spiritual needs as well. Mothers are famous for taking physical care of their children, but they must go beyond nursing aches and pains and share spiritual truths too. In 2 Timothy 1:5, look at a committed spiritual tag-team made up of a mother and a grandmother.

What were their names, and who was the object of their spiritual sensitivity and teaching (verse 2)?

In 2 Timothy 3:15, what does the apostle Paul say about the vital contribution made by these two women in Timothy's early life?

If you're a mom, you wouldn't dare fail to feed your children. But are you also giving them the spiritual food they need? What more can you do for their spiritual growth? (And P.S., every child can be spiritually influenced by a godly aunt and grandmother too!)

Reflecting the Heart of Jesus

Read this final section in your book again. As you consider your character, jot down two or three changes or actions that would cause you to be more sensitive to people and better reflect the heart of Jesus.

⁓ A Prayer to Pray ⁓

What can you add to the prayer in your book that will more specifically describe your desire to be more sensitive?

Day 24

A Servant

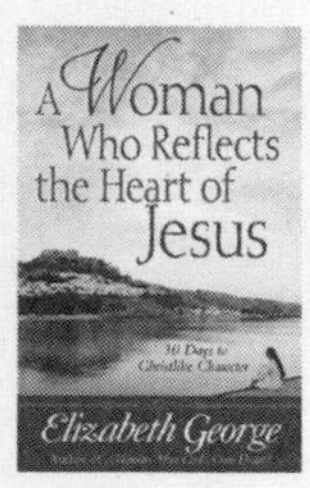

In your copy of *A Woman Who Reflects the Heart of Jesus*, read the chapter entitled "A Servant." What encouraged you the most about your journey to Christlike character, and why?

What challenged you the most, and why?

Jesus Shows Us the Way

As you read in your book, the prophet Isaiah often referred to the coming Messiah as God's "Servant." As you begin, copy these verses from your Bible:

Isaiah 42:1—

Isaiah 52:13—

Isaiah 53:11—

Seek First the Kingdom of God

According to Matthew 22:37-38, what is your first priority?

And your second (verse 39)?

For most women serving is a given. What is one of the biggest problems when it comes to serving, and why?

How do these verses from Colossians 3 help you to put all your serving and service into perspective?

Verse 23—

Verse 24—

What can you do to ensure that your list of priorities matches those God has set for you?

You Cannot Serve God and Mammon

After reading Luke 16:1-13, describe why you cannot serve two masters.

Look over the questions in this section. Do you see yourself having divided interests in any of the areas mentioned? Which ones?

How can you move serving God to the forefront of your heart, thoughts, and daily to-do list?

Reflecting On Your Heart

Make a list of your most cherished possessions. Are there any things on that list you couldn't let go of? If so, ask God to give you a neutral heart about these things. "Remember, if you can't let go of your possessions, you don't own them, they own you!"

The Son of Man Came to Serve

Read the words of Jesus in Matthew 20:25-28. What was His message about greatness and serving in...

verse 25?

verse 26?

verse 27?

How did Jesus describe Himself and His service in verse 28?

Paul was a powerful leader. Scan 1 Thessalonians 2:6-12. Pick out several ways the great apostle Paul demonstrated a servant's heart.

Reflecting On Your Heart

"Be Christlike—be a loving servant." After looking at Proverbs 31:20 and 1 Timothy 5:10 in your Bible, think of some ways you can further develop a servant spirit.

You Are Worried and Troubled About Many Things

What a joy to look again at the sisters, Martha and Mary! Once again, comb through Luke 10:38-42. Then take some time to evaluate your heart's focus. Mary served too, but Martha allowed her service to distract her from centering on Jesus. What are some of the "many things" that are distracting you from serving Jesus?

What steps can you take to follow Mary's example to ensure that you have "chosen that good part"—the Jesus part?

Reflecting On Your Heart

Serving others was at the core of Jesus' earthly ministry. This book is about reflecting the heart of Jesus. Therefore, serving others in the body of Christ should be at the core of your ministry. Not only do you have the greatest example of serving others in Jesus, who said, "Do as I have done to you" (John 13:15), but you also have a great command to "serve one another" (Galatians 5:13). Where is your heart? What are you doing to be a servant to your family, friends, church, and community?

Reflecting the Heart of Jesus

Read this final section in your book again. As you consider your character, jot down two or three changes or actions that would cause you to be a servant to people and better reflect the heart of Jesus.

~ A Prayer to Pray ~

What can you add to the prayer in your book that will more specifically describe your desire to be more of a servant?

Day 25

Submissive

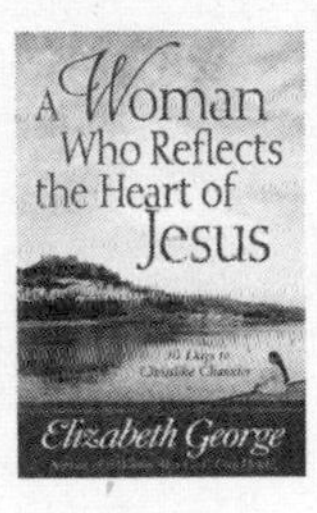

In your copy of *A Woman Who Reflects the Heart of Jesus*, read the chapter entitled "Submissive." What encouraged you the most about your journey to Christlike character, and why?

What challenged you the most, and why?

Jesus Shows Us the Way

Look up the words *submit, submission*, and *submissive* in a dictionary and write out a definition that helps you get a handle on the important character quality of submissiveness. Jot down any initial thoughts.

After reading this section in your book, what lessons did you learn regarding submission from Jesus' example?

Children, Obey Your Parents

Look at Luke 2:51 in your Bible. What choice did Jesus, the perfect Son of God (and the perfect child!), make at this time?

Jesus' obedience in the home surely contributed to His heavenly Father's praise of Him in Matthew 3:17—what did the Father say in that passage?

Key verses for both parents and children are found in Ephesians 6:1-4. Why is it important for children to heed the command in verse 1?

Bonus question: Submitting to people goes way beyond children and their parents. Jot down some other relationships in which submission is part of God's plan:

Ephesians 5:21—

Ephesians 5:22—

Ephesians 6:5—

1 Peter 5:5—

Hebrews 13:7,17—

Honor Your Father and Your Mother

Read Ephesians 6:1-3 and describe the difference between "obey" and "honor" as it applies to your role with your parents whether living or dead. (And here's a thought question: What message are you sending to your children when they see you honoring your parents?)

Now look at John 19:25-27. What lesson does Jesus' last request while hanging on the cross convey to you about your own parents?

If You Love Me, Keep My Commandments

To reflect the heart of Jesus means to obey all that God commands in the Bible. That's what Jesus did in Matthew 3:13-17. After reading these verses, realize that Jesus did not need to be baptized, yet He was obedient and submissive to "fulfill all righteousness" (verse 15). Now read Jesus' words to His disciples and all believers in John 14:15. Based on Jesus' words, how can you prove your love for Him?

Reflecting On Your Heart

"If you're feeling a little distant in your relationship with your Savior, perhaps it's because there's an area of submission that you're choosing to disregard." To get your heart right—and mend your relationship with Jesus—it's vital that you do the exercises suggested in your book: Take some time to search your heart. Be honest...and be submissive.

Live by Every Word from the Mouth of God

No one has ever been tempted as much as Jesus was. Therefore there is no one who can better teach you how to handle life and temptation than Jesus. Read Matthew 4:1-11 for yourself. How does submission to God's Word strengthen you to live God's way (verse 4)?

Reflecting On Your Heart

It's easy to memorize Bible verses, but "to be truly effective you are to submit to God's Word, not just quote it." See James 1:22 in your Bible and write it here. Is yours a heart that delights in doing what the Word says? Is yours a heart that willingly—and quickly—submits to the Word? If you're doing okay, keep on keeping on! If you're not doing so well, what will you "do" about it?

Is It Lawful to Pay Taxes?

Read Romans 13:1-7 and list several reasons you are to submit to higher authorities such as the government.

According to verses 6 and 7, how does this submission express itself in practice?

Take Up Your Cross and Follow Jesus

Be sure you read these powerful scriptures from your Bible. Then note what's involved in truly following Jesus.

Matthew 16:24—

Luke 14:27—

Reflecting On Your Heart

"Jesus isn't interested in a casual relationship with you, and He won't take a backseat to anything or anyone." What or who is standing in the way of you loving Him with all your heart and following Him with all your strength...and what will you do about it?

Not As I Will, but As You Will

Oh dear! It's time to read Genesis 3:1-7. How did Eve do her own will instead of submitting to God's clear and simple instructions?

Here are some key verses to learn by heart to help you do God's will. Write them out in your favorite translation, praise God for Jesus' submission to the Father's will (which secured your salvation), memorize the verses, and live by them!

John 4:34—

John 5:30—

Matthew 26:39—

Reflecting the Heart of Jesus

Read this final section in your book again. As you consider your character, jot down two or three changes or actions that would cause you to be more submissive and better reflect the heart of Jesus.

~ A Prayer to Pray ~

What can you add to the prayer in your book that will more specifically describe your desire to be more submissive?

Day 26

Thankful

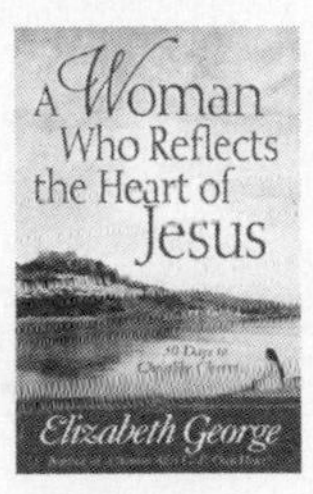

In your copy of *A Woman Who Reflects the Heart of Jesus*, read the chapter entitled "Thankful." What encouraged you the most about your journey to Christlike character, and why?

What challenged you the most, and why?

Jesus Shows Us the Way

Read 2 Corinthians 9:15, where the apostle Paul suggests that thanksgiving is appropriate in light of God's grace in salvation. How does Paul refer to this grace?

What thanks can you offer up to God for His work in your life?

He Must Increase

Expressing thankfulness and appreciation for others can be hard when those people are doing a better job than you are or have been promoted and you've been left behind. But this was not the case for John the Baptist. Read John 3:22-30 and key in on verses 28 and 30. How did John reveal his support of Jesus in verse 30?

Has there ever been a time when your ego was threatened because of someone else's qualifications? At the time, were you thankful and glad for that person? Having seen John's example of better behavior, how might you handle a similar situation differently today?

Thankfulness is a matter of the heart...and a shining character quality. How can you work on developing thankfulness as a habit, as an automatic response?

Reflecting On Your Heart

"Is there anyone in one of your ministries or at your workplace who has talents and abilities you don't possess?" Thank God for that person now. Give her encouragement and support. Even write down some things you can do to help her.

There Has Not Risen One Greater

In this section in your book you learned that John the Baptist prophesied regarding the coming of Jesus, the Messiah. When others wanted to exalt John, he pointed them to one greater, to Jesus. What did Jesus later tell the people about John in Matthew 11:9-11?

These two men formed a mutual admiration society. They were not in competition against each other. They were not jealous of each other. They were not threatened by each other. Instead, they were thankful for each other and there to help one another. Who at your workplace or at church, or even at home, is doing a good job? Be thankful! Let that person know that you've noticed and appreciate her efforts. Then see how many ways you can assist her.

Reflecting On Your Heart

Don't "forget what others have done and sacrificed and contributed to help you get where you are today." If you haven't already done it, create a gratitude list of the people who have mentored you and helped you get to where you are today. Thank God for them and plan to thank them personally—soon! Thankfulness was important to Jesus; therefore it should be important to you. Summarize the scene in Luke 17:11-19 here.

I Thank You, Father

Jesus was in a constant state of thankfulness—so much so that He was ever thankful to the Father. Read Matthew 11:20-26. What was happening here, and for what was Jesus thankful in this situation?

The apostle Paul, too, was always giving thanks. Look at several scriptures that will hopefully cause you to see thankfulness as your only and always option for responding to all situations, good or bad. Write out what the people in these verses were thankful for:

Romans 16:3-4—

Colossians 1:3—

1 Thessalonians 1:2-3—

1 Thessalonians 5:18—

Reflecting On Your Heart

"Take a page out of Jesus' life and be thankful," even for events that are difficult or impossible to understand. Resist the urge to question God's actions, blame others, or become bitter. How does Jesus' thankful response to rejection help you to deal with your own hard-to-understand issues?

Thank You that You Have Heard Me

Read John 11:39-42 and share why it is important that people hear your thankfulness expressed in your conversations and in your prayers (verse 42).

Reflecting On Your Heart

"Thank God that He hears your prayers." This fact should encourage you to pray—often and about everything! Where will you start? Who needs your prayers? What matters are urgent?

And when will you start?

Be faithful. Be committed. And be verbal. God is glorified when you pray…and He answers prayer!

Reflecting a Thankful Spirit

You'll want to take time to read devotionally and reverently through the magnificent prayer in John 17—a prayer from the heart of Jesus. But for now, skim through John 17 and pick out three or four phrases that reveal Jesus' thankfulness.

Now jot down three or four things you are thankful for.

—

—

—

—

Reflecting the Heart of Jesus

Read this final section in your book again. As you consider your character, jot down two or three changes or actions that would cause you to be more thankful and better reflect the heart of Jesus.

~ A Prayer to Pray ~

What can you add to the prayer in your book that will more specifically describe your desire to be more thankful?

Day 27

Truthful

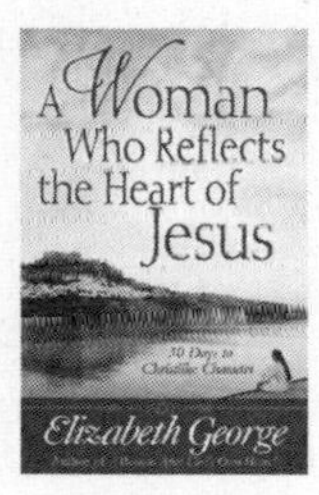

In your copy of *A Woman Who Reflects the Heart of Jesus*, read the chapter entitled "Truthful." What encouraged you the most about your journey to Christlike character, and why?

What challenged you the most, and why?

The Truth About Truth

In your own words, summarize the truths taught in the following verses from your favorite Bible translation.

Titus 1:2—

John 1:14—

John 14:6—

John 14:16-17—

John 17:17—

What do these verses teach you about trusting God and His Word, the Bible?

Do you have a favorite truth from the Bible? Write it out and be faithful to share it with others. Everyone can use encouragement.

The Warning About Lies

Look at the verses in this section of your book. Did you learn anything new?

How do these verses reveal the seriousness of lying?

Which ones got a little too close for comfort?

What is the number one change you are going to make in the area of telling the truth?

Jesus Shows Us the Way

I Tell You the Truth

First read John 8:45. In addition to this verse, what do the following scriptures teach about the devil or Satan and those associated with him?

Acts 5:3—

Acts 13:10—

Revelation 12:9

How do the verses above speak to you about staying close to Jesus?

Reflecting On Your Heart

"Lying has no place in a child of God." How do these words pierce your heart, and what are your plans to be a woman of truth?

Let Your Yes Be Yes, and Your No, No

Matthew 5:34-37 has a lot to say about telling the truth. What do the following verses communicate?

Verses 34-36—

Verse 37—

What is God's bottom line on swearing in verse 37?

Putting Away Lying

What does Ephesians 4:24 say about you as a Christian?

Therefore, according to Ephesians 4:25, what has to be completely eliminated from your life?

Speaking the Truth in Love

Throughout this book we have majored on Christlike behavior and being like Jesus. How does following the admonition in Ephesians 4:15 help make this happen?

Be Not Slanderers

Here are a couple verses that speak specifically to women. What is the message of…

1 Timothy 3:11?

Titus 2:3?

Quickly review the scriptures in this study on truthfulness. What is your plan for ensuring Christlikeness in your speech?

Reflecting the Heart of Jesus

Read this final section in your book again. As you consider your character, jot down two or three changes or actions that would cause you to be more truthful to people and better reflect the heart of Jesus.

~ A Prayer to Pray ~

What can you add to the prayer in your book that will more specifically describe your desire to be more truthful?

Day 28

Virtuous

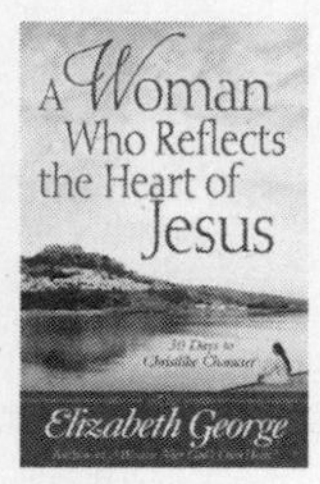

In your copy of *A Woman Who Reflects the Heart of Jesus*, read the chapter entitled "Virtuous." What encouraged you the most about your journey to Christlike character, and why?

What challenged you the most, and why?

Discovering the Meaning of Virtuous

Read again the quote from *Beautiful in God's Eyes* (on page 234 of your book). What did you learn about the meaning of the word *virtuous?*

How does its definition strengthen and fortify you for your many responsibilities?

Jesus Shows Us the Way

I Am Well Pleased

Read Luke 2:52 and list the areas of Jesus' life that were affected as He matured.

Which two of these areas are also addressed in the meaning of *virtuous* (see above)?

Reflecting On Your Heart

"Excellence is a process. It doesn't happen overnight. There is a course of action involved...you are a work in progress." How do these words encourage you to keep moving forward in your maturing process, in your pursuit of excellence and virtue?

He Has Done All Things Well

List the different types of healing Jesus did in Mark 7:24-37.

Verses 24-30—

Verses 31-36—

What was the observation and conclusion of the people who witnessed these miracles (verse 37)?

Now read the parable of the talents in Matthew 25:14-30. What responsibility was given to the servants in the parable?

When the master returned, what was his commendation of the first two servants?

What did the master have to say about the third servant?

What does this parable teach you about your own life and God's view of the quality of virtuousness or excellence?

Reflecting On Your Heart

"As a Christian, excellence is to be your goal in every area and every role of your life." Can you point to a few areas in which you excel, in which you are truly doing well? Note them now and thank God for His grace.

Can you point to a few areas in which you need improvement, areas you may be neglecting or in which you are taking a few shortcuts? List one or two areas and jot down how you plan to tackle them and turn them around.

You Shall Receive Power

Read Galatians 5:22-23. The fruit of the Spirit is like a rainbow—one rainbow made up of many colors (or, for us, qualities!). List the fruit of the Spirit here.

—	—	—
—	—	—
—	—	—

Circle the quality that needs your attention right away so you can continue your growth into a woman of excellence. Be sure any steps you want to take are recorded onto your prayer list and into your planner!

Reflecting On Your Heart

"Whatever you do in word or deed, do all in the name of the Lord Jesus." How do these words show you the way to Christlike conduct?

Reflecting the Heart of Jesus

Read this final section in your book again. As you consider your character, jot down two or three changes or actions that would cause you to be more virtuous and better reflect the heart of Jesus.

~ A Prayer to Pray ~

What can you add to the prayer in your book that will more specifically describe your desire to be more virtuous?

Day 29

Wise

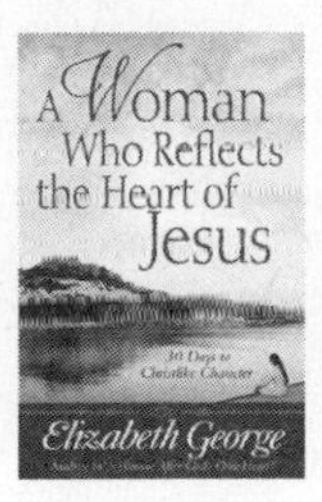

In your copy of *A Woman Who Reflects the Heart of Jesus*, read the chapter entitled "Wise." What gave you the most encouragement for your journey to Christ-like character, and why?

What challenged you the most, and why?

Jesus Shows Us the Way

The Source of All Wisdom

Want wisdom? Start with Proverbs 1:5. What actions and efforts will a wise person take to get wisdom and understanding?

—

—

—

What does Proverbs 1:7 say about the source of wisdom?

What does Proverbs 9:10 add to this information?

Based on these teachings, what actions are missing in your quest to increase in wisdom?

The Path to True Wisdom

Scan John 3:1-17, a conversation between the man Nicodemus, an Old Testament scholar, and Jesus. How does Proverbs 9:9 describe a man like Nicodemus?

According to verse 10, what is the path toward true wisdom?

Reflecting On Your Heart

"As you understand and accept the concept of being born again, wisdom becomes yours in Jesus Christ." Jesus is asking you, "Have you been born again and received eternal life through Me?" If you have, praise God and continue to seek His wisdom. If not, be sure you consider John 1:12 and 14:6. And don't forget to do what Proverbs 1:5 says—seek wise counsel from a Christian friend or pastor.

The Quest for Wisdom

In your Bible read Proverbs 2:1-6, and jot down the many efforts involved in gaining wisdom.

What kind of energy are you expending to get wisdom? Describe the ways you sought wisdom during the past 24 hours.

Did you do well, or did your answer reveal an "Oops!"? Be sure to make a quick plan here for doing better tomorrow.

Search the Scriptures

Psalm 119 is a fascinating portion of Scripture. Did you know some reference is made to the Word of God in every one of its 176 verses? Read it...and you will hunger and thirst for God's Word! What do these verses in Psalm 119 say about the wisdom that comes from the Word of God?

Verse 98—

Verse 99—

Verse 100—

What was the psalmist's passion toward the Word of God in verse 97?

Now make another list: According to 2 Timothy 3:16-17, what are some of the benefits of the Scriptures? (Hint: Try to find six or seven.)

Reflecting On Your Heart

"Getting to know Jesus by reading the Bible will give you the knowledge you need to make wise decisions [and] better choices." What's facing you today or in the week to come that requires a decision? Note it here, pray, and search the Scriptures.

Ask of God

What quick principles for prayer do you find in Matthew 7:7-8?

	Your Responsibility	*God's Result*
—		
—		
—		

After reading about Solomon, what lessons can you take to heart in your efforts to gain wisdom?

After reading about Rehoboam, what mistakes do you need to avoid in your decision-making process?

Reflecting On Your Heart

"You don't have a kingdom to run, but you do have a household, your family, your finances, and your life to run." In short, you need wisdom! How do you plan to get the wisdom you need?

Get Wisdom

Many voices are telling you to get wisdom. For another voice, look at Luke 2:52. What do you learn here about Jesus and His process for becoming wise?

What is God's instruction to you in Proverbs 4:7?

Write out the four steps presented in your book. (Don't forget the most important step—look at each verse in your Bible.)

Step #1—Proverbs 3:13-14

Step #2—Proverbs 2:3,5

Step #3—Proverbs 2:4

Step #4—Proverbs 3:5-6

Your assignment? Make a plan to apply all four steps this week. You can write it here, or in your planner, or prayer book, or on a note you put on your refrigerator door.

Reflecting the Heart of Jesus

Read this final section in your book again. As you consider your character, jot down two or three changes or actions that would cause you to be more wise and better reflect the heart of Jesus.

~ A Prayer to Pray ~

What can you add to the prayer in your book that will more specifically describe your desire to grow more wise?

Day 30

Worshipful

In your copy of *A Woman Who Reflects the Heart of Jesus*, read the chapter entitled "Worshipful." What encouraged you the most about your journey to Christlike character, and why?

What challenged you the most, and why?

Jesus Shows Us the Way

When you think of worship, what comes to your mind?

Now scan through this section in your book and jot down some of the ways Jesus worshiped.

They Presented Gifts to Him

Here are several more scenes and means of worship. First, look at the wise men in Matthew 2:9-11 in your Bible. In addition to tremendous dedication and great effort, how did these men worship and honor Jesus, according to verse 11?

Next read Genesis 4:1-5. Here you are treated to a vivid contrast of worship—and hearts—in two brothers. What did Cain bring to the Lord (verse 3), and what did Abel offer (verse 4)?

How did God respond (verses 4 and 5)?

Now read Romans 12:1 and then describe another offering you can bring to God in worship. Write out the qualifiers that make this offering acceptable to God.

Reflecting On Your Heart

Your worship involves your best—"your best attitude, your best praise, your best obedience, your best-chosen heartfelt adoration, and your best self." Can you think of ways to make your worship better? Note several ways here. And, of course, apply them!

She Gave Thanks to the Lord

Read Luke 2:36-38. This dear lady lived to worship! Where did Anna reside (verse 37)?

How did she worship (verse 37)?

When did she worship (verse 37)?

Because she was worshiping in the right place at the right time, how was she blessed (verse 38)?

What was her worshipful response (verse 38)?

Reflecting On Your Heart

Anna remained at the temple constantly. By contrast, you are free to worship and offer praise to the Lord anywhere at any time. "The more you are aware of His presence, the more you'll want to pray and praise Him." You can worship God anywhere because He is omnipresent. You can worship God within your heart because He is omniscient. You can worship God with your petitions because He is omnipotent. How can you get started? Resolve to follow the example of the psalmist in Psalm 146:1-2.

Worship in Spirit and Truth

To launch this topic, read John 4:23-24. Now think back on your last formal worship experience. Where were you? What was your attitude when you arrived...and during the service? Were you changed in any way as a result of your worship?

As you recall your heart and your time at worship, do you think you were worshiping in spirit? Why or why not?

And do you think you were worshiping in truth?

Reflecting On Your Heart

"Before you worship again, search your heart." How should (and will) you approach your next opportunity for formal worship?

Hear Him

Read about the dazzling, thrilling, miraculous scene that occurred in Matthew 17:1-5. Note the place, list the people who were there, and tell what took place (verses 1-3).

Sometimes it's hard to know how to handle the unusual—so we talk. That's what Peter did. But who cut him off, and what corrective instruction was given (verse 5)?

It's obvious that hearing the Word and obeying the Word constitutes authentic worship. A woman who desires to reflect the character of Jesus is a woman whose ongoing prayer is to obey God. Search your heart. Is there any object, person, or area in your life where obedience is not occurring? Talk it over with God now and determine what you will do about it.

Reflecting the Heart of Jesus

Please reread this section again. As you consider your own character, what specific actions do you need to take so you can better reflect the heart of Jesus in the area of being more worshipful?

~ A Praise to Offer ~

Read again the section entitled "A Praise to Offer." Also, take your Bible in hand and read Revelation 5:11-14. Jesus is to be the object of your worship, and all angelic beings and believers throughout time are to worship Jesus, the Lamb who was slain. Don't wait until you get to heaven to offer praise, adoration, and worship to your Savior, Christ the Lord.

Leading a Bible Study Discussion Group

What a privilege it is to lead a Bible study! And what joy and excitement await you as you delve into the Word of God and help others to discover its life-changing truths. If God has called you to lead a Bible study group, I know you'll be spending much time in prayer and planning and giving much thought to being an effective leader. I also know that taking the time to read through the following tips will help you to navigate the challenges of leading a Bible study discussion group and enjoying the effort and opportunity.

The Leader's Roles

As a Bible study group leader, you'll find your role changing back and forth from *expert* to *cheerleader* to *lover* to *referee* during the course of a session.

Since you're the leader, group members will look to you to be the *expert* guiding them through the material. So be well prepared. In fact, be over-prepared so that you know the material better than any group member does. Start your study early in the week and let its message simmer all week long. (You might even work several lessons ahead so that you have in mind the big picture and the overall direction of the study.) Be ready to share some additional gems that your group members wouldn't have discovered on their own. That extra insight from your study time—or that comment from a wise Bible teacher or scholar, that clever saying, that keen observation from another believer, and even an appropriate joke—adds an element of fun and keeps Bible study from becoming routine, monotonous, and dry.

Second, be ready to be the group's *cheerleader*. Your energy and enthusiasm for the task at hand can be contagious. It can also stimulate people to get more involved in their personal study as well as in the group discussion.

Third, be the *lover,* the one who shows a genuine concern for the members of the group. You're the one who will establish the atmosphere of the group. If you laugh and have fun, the group members will laugh and have fun. If you hug, they will hug. If you care, they will care. If you share, they will share. If you love, they will love. So pray every day to love the women God has placed in your group. Ask Him to show you how to love them with His love.

Finally, as the leader, you'll need to be the *referee* on occasion. That means making sure everyone has an equal opportunity to speak. That's easier to do when you operate under the assumption that every member of the group has something worthwhile to contribute. So, trusting that the Lord has taught each person during the week, act on that assumption.

Expert, cheerleader, lover, and referee—these four roles of the leader may make the task seem overwhelming. But that's not bad if it keeps you on your knees praying for your group.

A Good Start

Beginning on time, greeting people warmly, and opening in prayer gets the study off to a good start. Know what you want to have happen during your time together and make sure those things get done. That kind of order means comfort for those involved.

Establish a format and let the group members know what that format is. People appreciate being in a Bible study that focuses on the Bible. So keep the discussion on the topic and move the group through the questions. Tangents are often hard to avoid—and even harder to rein in. So be sure to focus on the answers to questions about the specific passage at hand. After all, the purpose of the group is Bible study!

Finally, as someone has accurately observed, "Personal growth is one of the by-products of any effective small group. This growth is achieved when people are recognized and accepted by others. The more friendliness, mutual trust, respect, and warmth exhibited, the more likely that the member will find pleasure in the group, and, too, the more likely she will work hard toward the accomplishment of the group's goals. The effective leader will strive to reinforce desirable traits" (source unknown).

A Dozen Helpful Tips

Here is a list of helpful suggestions for leading a Bible study discussion group:

1. Arrive early, ready to focus fully on others and give of yourself. If you have to do any last-minute preparation, review, regrouping, or praying, do it in the car. Don't dash in, breathless, harried, late, still tweaking your plans.
2. Check out your meeting place in advance. Do you have everything you need—tables, enough chairs, a blackboard, hymnals if you plan to sing, coffee, etc.?
3. Greet each person warmly by name as she arrives. After all, you've been praying for these women all week long, so let each VIP know that you're glad she's arrived.
4. Use name tags for at least the first two or three weeks.
5. Start on time no matter what—even if only one person is there!
6. Develop a pleasant but firm opening statement. You might say, "This lesson was great! Let's get started so we can enjoy all of it!" or "Let's pray before we begin our lesson."
7. Read the questions, but don't hesitate to reword them on occasion. Rather than reading an entire paragraph of instructions, for instance, you might say, "Question 1 asks us to list some ways that Christ displayed humility. Lisa, please share one way Christ displayed humility."
8. Summarize or paraphrase the answers given. Doing so will keep the discussion focused on the topic, eliminate digressions, help

avoid or clear up any misunderstandings of the text, and keep each group member aware of what the others are saying.

9. Keep moving and don't add any of your own questions to the discussion time. It's important to get through the study guide questions. So if a cut-and-dried answer is called for, you don't need to comment with anything other than a "thank you." But when the question asks for an opinion or an application (for instance, "How can this truth help us in our marriages?" or "How do *you* find time for your quiet time?"), let all who want to contribute.
10. Affirm each person who contributes, especially if the contribution was very personal, painful to share, or a quiet person's rare statement. Make everyone who shares a hero by saying something like "Thank you for sharing that insight from your own life" or "We certainly appreciate what God has taught you. Thank you for letting us in on it."
11. Watch your watch, put a clock right in front of you, or consider using a timer. Pace the discussion so that you meet your cut-off time, especially if you want time to pray. Stop at the designated time even if you haven't finished the lesson. Remember that everyone has worked through the study once; you are simply going over it again.
12. End on time. You can only make friends with your group members by ending on time or even a little early! Besides, members of your group have the next item on their agenda to attend to—picking up children from the nursery, babysitter, or school; heading home to tend to matters there; running errands; getting to bed; or spending some time with their husbands. So let them out *on time!*

Five Common Problems

In any group, you can anticipate certain problems. Here are some common ones that can arise, along with helpful solutions:

1. *The incomplete lesson*—Right from the start, establish the policy that if someone has not done the lesson, it is best for

her not to answer the questions. But do try to include her responses to questions that ask for opinions or experiences. Everyone can share some thoughts in reply to a question like, "Reflect on what you know about both athletic and spiritual training and then share what you consider to be the essential elements of training oneself in godliness."

2. *The gossip*—The Bible clearly states that gossiping is wrong, so you don't want to allow it in your group. Set a high and strict standard by saying, "I am not comfortable with this conversation," or "We [not *you*] are gossiping, ladies. Let's move on."

3. *The talkative member*—Here are three scenarios and some possible solutions for each.

    a. The problem talker may be talking because she has done her homework and is excited about something she has to share. She may also know more about the subject than the others and, if you cut her off, the rest of the group may suffer.

    Solution: Respond with a comment like: "Sarah, you are making very valuable contributions. Let's see if we can get some reactions from the others," or "I know Sarah can answer this. She's really done her homework. How about some of the rest of you?"

    b. The talkative member may be talking because she has *not* done her homework and wants to contribute, but she has no boundaries.

    Solution: Establish at the first meeting that those who have not done the lesson do not contribute except on opinion or application questions. You may need to repeat this guideline at the beginning of each session.

    c. The talkative member may want to be heard whether or not she has anything worthwhile to contribute.

    Solution: After subtle reminders, be more direct, saying, "Betty, I know you would like to share your ideas, but let's give others a chance. I'll call on you later."

4. *The quiet member*—Here are two scenarios and possible solutions.

    a. The quiet member wants the floor but somehow can't get the chance to share.

    SOLUTION: Clear the path for the quiet member by first watching for clues that she wants to speak (moving to the edge of her seat, looking as if she wants to speak, perhaps even starting to say something) and then saying, "Just a second. I think Chris wants to say something." Then, of course, make her a hero!

    b. The quiet member simply doesn't want the floor.

    SOLUTION: "Chris, what answer do you have on question 2?" or "Chris, what do you think about…?" Usually after a shy person has contributed a few times, she will become more confident and more ready to share. Your role is to provide an opportunity where there is *no* risk of a wrong answer. But occasionally a group member will tell you that she would rather not be called on. Honor her request, but from time to time ask her privately if she feels ready to contribute to the group discussions.

    In fact, give all your group members the right to pass. During your first meeting, explain that any time a group member does not care to share an answer, she may simply say, "I pass." You'll want to repeat this policy at the beginning of every group session.

5. *The wrong answer*—Never tell a group member that she has given a wrong answer, but at the same time never let a wrong answer go by.

    SOLUTION: Either ask if someone else has a different answer or ask additional questions that will cause the right answer to emerge. As the women get closer to the right answer, say, "We're getting warmer! Keep thinking! We're almost there!"

Learning from Experience

Immediately after each Bible study session, evaluate the group discussion time using this checklist. You may also want a member of your group (or an assistant or trainee or outside observer) to evaluate you periodically.

May God strengthen—and encourage!—you as you assist others in the discovery of His many wonderful truths.

Personal Notes

Personal Notes

Personal Notes

Personal Notes

Personal Notes

Personal Notes

Personal Notes

Personal Notes

Personal Notes

Personal Notes

About the Author

Elizabeth George is a bestselling author who has more than 5 million books in print and is a popular speaker at Christian women's events. Her passion is to teach the Bible in a way that changes women's lives.

For information about Elizabeth's speaking ministry or to purchase her books visit her website:

www.ElizabethGeorge.com

or call 1-800-542-4611

Elizabeth George
PO Box 2879
Belfair, WA 98528

Books by Elizabeth George

- Beautiful in God's Eyes
- Breaking the Worry Habit...Forever
- Finding God's Path Through Your Trials
- Following God with All Your Heart
- Life Management for Busy Women
- Loving God with All Your Mind
- A Mom After God's Own Heart
- Quiet Confidence for a Woman's Heart
- The Remarkable Women of the Bible
- Small Changes for a Better Life
- Walking with the Women of the Bible
- A Wife After God's Own Heart
- Windows into the Word of God
- A Woman After God's Own Heart®
- A Woman After God's Own Heart® Deluxe Edition
- A Woman After God's Own Heart®—A Daily Devotional
- A Woman After God's Own Heart® Collection
- A Woman After God's Own Heart® DVD and Workbook
- A Woman's Call to Prayer
- A Woman's High Calling
- A Woman's Walk with God
- A Woman Who Reflects the Heart of Jesus
- A Young Woman After God's Own Heart
- A Young Woman After God's Own Heart—A Devotional
- A Young Woman's Call to Prayer
- A Young Woman's Guide to Making Right Choices
- A Young Woman's Walk with God

Study Guides

- Beautiful in God's Eyes Growth & Study Guide
- Finding God's Path Through Your Trials Growth & Study Guide
- Following God with All Your Heart Growth & Study Guide
- Life Management for Busy Women Growth & Study Guide
- Loving God with All Your Mind Growth & Study Guide
- A Mom After God's Own Heart Growth & Study Guide
- The Remarkable Women of the Bible Growth & Study Guide
- Small Changes for a Better Life Growth & Study Guide
- A Wife After God's Own Heart Growth & Study Guide
- A Woman After God's Own Heart® Growth & Study Guide
- A Woman's Call to Prayer Growth & Study Guide
- A Woman's High Calling Growth & Study Guide
- A Woman's Walk with God Growth & Study Guide

Children's Books

- A Girl After God's Own Heart
- God's Wisdom for Little Girls
- A Little Girl After God's Own Heart

Books by Jim & Elizabeth George

- God Loves His Precious Children
- God's Wisdom for Little Boys
- A Little Boy After God's Own Heart

Books by Jim George

- The Bare Bones Bible® Handbook
- The Bare Bones Bible® Handbook for Teens
- The Bare Bones Bible® Bios
- The Bare Bones Bible® Facts
- A Husband After God's Own Heart
- A Man After God's Own Heart
- The Man Who Makes a Difference
- The Remarkable Prayers of the Bible
- A Young Man After God's Own Heart